❧ *The Autobiographical*
  Myth of
  ROBERT LOWELL

The Autobiographical Myth of ROBERT LOWELL

by <u>Philip Cooper</u>

The University of North Carolina Press
Chapel Hill

~ PREFACE

~ My purpose is to explore the coherence of Robert Lowell's poetry as a single body. Lowell himself has said, "All your poems are in a sense one poem." The principle of their interrelation governs the change of poetic style represented in *Life Studies,* and throughout his work transforms personal materials into autobiographical myth. In its moment of emergence that myth takes lyric form, but its cumulative pattern reaches, in Lowell's most recent work, beyond the received boundaries of the lyric genre.

Lowell's friend Randall Jarrell, reviewing *Lord Weary's Castle* in 1947, made the pioneer study of the basic principle in Lowell's poems. There have been other notable studies since then, but along other lines; and since Lowell's work is still very much in progress, no one has been able to sample it all. Hugh B. Staples' *Robert Lowell: The First Twenty Years* (1962) ends with *Life Studies;* I concentrate mainly on the poems that have appeared since then. Jerome Mazzaro's book, *The Poetic Themes of Robert Lowell* (1965), has a Roman Catholic emphasis I do not follow. Irvin Ehrenpreis's valuable essay, "The Age of Lowell" (1965), was written before the appearance of *For the Union Dead,* and M. L. Rosenthal's extensive treatment of Robert Lowell in *The New Poets* (1967) was written before the appearance of *Near the Ocean.* The excellent, synoptic essay-review by Daniel Hoffman, "Robert Lowell's *Near the Ocean:* The Greatness and Horror of Empire" (1967), despite its title, is concerned more with the plays than with the poems. My purpose is to demonstrate the principle governing the poems. The closest to what I propose is Gabriel Pearson's essay, "Robert Lowell," in *The Review* for March, 1969. It is a sensitive essay in every respect, but I find it particularly useful for its understanding of Lowell's so-called confessional mode, a subject on which that essay and this book converge. "In explicitly treating his life as materials," Mr. Pearson writes, "he was not making his poetry more personal but depersonalising his own life." Properly considered, Lowell's confessional mode is not other than the principle of poetry itself: the personal touches the archetypal, becoming autobiographical myth.

I want to thank R. J. Kaufmann, Richard M. Gollin, G. S. Fraser, John Rees Moore, Louis D. Rubin, and Julia Randall, who read my manuscript in various stages, and helped me to make it better. I am also grateful to Mary Louise Zaidel and the staff of the library at the University of Maryland, Baltimore County, as well as to Shirley Henn and the staff of the library at Hollins College, for their cheerful, skillful uncovering of facts and materials whenever I wanted them.

✍ CONTENTS

~ A CHRONOLOGICAL LIST
OF ABBREVIATIONS

LOU	Land of Unlikeness	1944
LWC	Lord Weary's Castle	1946
MK	The Mills of the Kavanaughs	1951
LS	Life Studies	1959
PHAEDRA	Phaedra and Figaro	1961
IMIT	Imitations	1961
FUD	For the Union Dead	1964
OG	The Old Glory	1965
NO	Near the Ocean	1967
PB	Prometheus Bound	1969
NBK	Notebook 1967–68	1969

~ *The Autobiographical*
Myth of
ROBERT LOWELL

ᕈ *I. INTRODUCTION*

I am a worshipper of myth and monster.

ᕈOne of Robert Lowell's most famous poems, "The Quaker Graveyard in Nantucket," refers to its blue sailors as "sea-monsters, upward angel, downward fish" (LWC). The figure echoes Milton's image of Dagon, the fallen angel: "sea monster, upward man / And downward fish" (*Paradise Lost*, I, 462–3). It is also related to King Lear's image of his daughters, or fallen man: "But to the girdle do the gods inherit, / Beneath is all the fiends'," Lear says (IV, vi, 128). A few scenes earlier, Albany cries out:

> *Tigers, not daughters, what have you performed?*
> *. . . If that the Heavens do not their visible spirits*
> *Send quickly down to tame these vile offenses,*
> *It will come.*
> *Humanity must perforce prey on itself,*
> *Like monsters of the deep* (IV, ii, 40).

Albany develops a figure of Lear's, from Lear's speech to Albany and Goneril in Act I:

> *Ingratitude! thou marble-hearted fiend,*
> *More hideous when thou show'st thee in a child*
> *Than the sea-monster* (I, iv, 281).

The sea-monsters, the monsters of the deep, make a figure of mindless rapacity, unspeakable inhumanity; but the figure

3

depends, for its poetic force, upon its collocation with human-ity, with the god-like or angelic aspect of the human condi-tion. The elemental ambivalence of the blue sailors in "The Quaker Graveyard in Nantucket," like that of human behavior as a whole in King Lear, comprises the thematic equivalent of a formal principle, a principle governing Lowell's poems. Lowell has mastered opposite extremes of style; he has ex-plored both literary density and conversational nonchalance; yet in spite of its diverseness, his work is unusually unified, as a body. "All your poems are in a sense one poem,"[1] Lowell himself has said. To understand how that can be is the critical problem. The recurrence of a radical thematic ambivalence, epitomized by what we may call Lowell's monster, and the ubiquity of its correlative formal principle, ambivalence as lyric structure, are like two threads of a single clue, to be followed in this study of Lowell's poems.

~~~~~~~~~~~~~~~~~

Lowell began in the grand manner. Land of Unlikeness (1944), Lord Weary's Castle (1946), and The Mills of the Kavanaughs (1951) are full of poems in which Dylan Thomas, Hopkins, and even Milton would feel at home.[2] "Chil-

1. Robert Lowell, in an interview with Frederic Seidel, "Robert Lowell," in Writers at Work: The Paris Review Interviews, Second Series (New York: The Viking Press, 1963), p. 349.
2. Robert Lowell, Land of Unlikeness (Cummington, Mass.: The Cum-mington Press, 1944), an edition of 250 copies, is out of print; about a third of the poems reappear in Lord Weary's Castle (New York: Harcourt, Brace & Co., 1946), which is for all practical purposes Lowell's first volume. His next volumes are Poems: 1938–1949 (London: Faber and Faber, 1950) and The Mills of the Kavanaughs (New York: Harcourt, Brace & Co., 1951). In the latter volume the new poems in the Faber volume are reprinted and the long title poem, which was not in the Faber volume, is added. All of these, except for the poems in Land of Unlikeness that were abandoned in Lord Weary's Castle, reappear in Lord Weary's Castle and The Mills of the Kavanaughs (New York: Meridian Books, 1961), which is the volume I have used.
   For the chronology and other details of Lowell's publishings up to Sep-tember 1, 1961, Hugh B. Staples, Robert Lowell: The First Twenty Years (New York: Farrar, Straus & Cudahy, 1962), has an indispensable bibli-ography (pp. 108–15). Jerome Mazzaro, The Achievement of Robert Lowell: 1939–1959 (Detroit: University of Detroit Press, 1960), is all bibliography; it "seems especially useful for finding reviews of Lowell's

dren of Light," for instance, in both of the first two volumes, has something of the density of sound, and the outrage, even the same echo of Jeremiah (the stocks and stones), that characterize Milton's sonnet "On the Late Massacre in Piedmont."[3] Then in the fifties (with Eliot, Frost, and William Carlos Williams, for example, as antecedents, and later with Allen Ginsberg and Elizabeth Bishop, for example, as models), Lowell began to move in the direction of *Life Studies* (1959),[4] with its extraordinarily down-to-earth style. The new way, which had its declared beginning in March, 1957,

---

books," writes Irvin Ehrenpreis in his own one-page bibliography prefacing his essay, "The Age of Lowell," in Irvin Ehrenpreis (ed.), *American Poetry* (London: Edward Arnold, 1965), p. 68. Mazzaro's more recent book, *The Poetic Themes of Robert Lowell* (Ann Arbor: University of Michigan Press, 1965), has a three-and-a-half-page bibliography (pp. 137–40).

3. Jerome Mazzaro (*ibid.*, p. 30) refers to "Children of Light" as "a satirical and pregnant poem the opening of which echoes lines from Milton's 'On the Late Massacre in Piedmont.' " "Massacres as well as wars," Mazzaro continues, "repeat themselves and both the Pilgrims and their descendants are Cain figures who formed the boundaries of their properties with murdered Redmen's bones." The question of echoes is incidental, of course, to my broader point that Lowell's poem in tone and style, in the more or less grand manner of its organization of speech, is somewhat comparable to Milton's sonnet. But I may add in passing that Milton's line, "When all our fathers worshipped stocks and stones," alludes in turn, as Douglas Bush points out (in *The Complete Poetical Works of John Milton*, ed. Douglas Bush [Boston: Houghton Mifflin Company, 1965], p. 198, note to line 4), to Jeremiah (2:26–27): "As the thief is ashamed when he is found, so is the house of Israel ashamed; they, their kings, their princes, and their priests, and their prophets, Saying to a stock, Thou art my father; and to a stone, Thou hast brought me forth. . . ."

Lowell's fifth line, "They planted here the Serpent's seeds of light," has affinities with Milton's tenth line, "Their martyred blood and ashes sow / O'er all th' Italian fields. . . ." Bush comments on Milton: "Cf. the parable of the sower (Matt: 13:3–9) and the myth of the warriors who sprang from the dragon's teeth sowed by Cadmus. The idea of the blood of martyrs as the seed of the church goes back at least to Tertullian, *Apologeticus* 50." (*Ibid.*)

4. The English edition of *Life Studies* (London: Faber and Faber, 1959) does not include "91 Revere Street," a thirty-five page autobiographical essay in prose which was first published in 1956 in *Partisan Review*. The essay is included in the American edition of *Life Studies* (New York: Farrar, Straus & Cudahy, 1959 [1960]). In the paperback edition an important poem, "Colonel Shaw and the Massachusetts' 54th," is added.

pressed into the sixties, shaping the work of *Imitations* (1961) as well as *For the Union Dead* (1964), *Near the Ocean* (1967), and *Notebook 1967–68*, but without permanently abandoning the traditional verse forms.[5]

It was the "Beat" fashion of coffee-house readings, together with his experiments in autobiographical prose—"91 Revere Street" first came out in 1956 (in *Partisan Review*), and "My Last Afternoon with Uncle Devereux Winslow" was written first in prose—that brought Lowell to change his style and get down off his stilts. Here is his own account:

> . . . I had been giving readings on the West Coast, often reading six days a week and sometimes twice in a single day. I was in San Francisco, the era and setting of Allen Ginsberg, and all about very modest poets were waking up prophets. I became sorely aware of how few poems I had written, and that these few had been finished at the latest three or four years earlier. Their style seemed distant, symbol-ridden and willfully difficult. I began to paraphrase my Latin quotations, and to add extra syllables to a line to make it clearer and more colloquial. I felt my old poems hid what they were really about, and many times offered a stiff, humorless and even impenetrable surface. I am no convert to the "beats." I know well too that the best poems are not necessarily poems that read aloud. Many of the greatest poems can only be read to one's self, for inspiration is no substitute for humor, shock, narrative and a hypnotic voice, the four musts for oral performance. Still, my own poems seemed like prehistoric monsters dragged down into the bog and death by their ponderous armor. I was reciting what I no longer felt. What influenced me more than San Francisco and reading aloud was that for some time I had been writing prose. I felt that the best style for poetry was none of the many poetic styles in English, but something like the prose of Chekhov or Flaubert.

5. Robert Lowell, *Imitations* (New York: Farrar, Straus & Cudahy, 1961), is a book of amazing translations. In *For the Union Dead* (New York: Farrar, Straus & Giroux, 1964) thirty-four new poems are added to the total work; this later volume is linked to *Life Studies* by the title poem, "For the Union Dead," which is "Colonel Shaw and the Massachusetts' 54th" renamed but substantially unchanged. *Near the Ocean* (New York: Farrar, Straus & Giroux, 1967) comprises seven new poems and nine translations. *The Voyage, and Other Versions of Poems by Baudelaire* (London: Faber and Faber, 1968) is a deluxe edition of the translations from Baudelaire in *Imitations*. *Notebook 1967–68* (New York: Farrar, Straus & Giroux, 1969), which Lowell asks to be regarded as one poem, consists of 274 sections, fourteen lines each.

When I returned to my home, I began writing lines in a new style.[6]

"Children of Light" (1944), which provides a brief example of the early style, may be contrasted with "The Mouth of the Hudson" (1964) to illustrate the revolution that has taken place. Both poems, moreover, illustrate the principle of ambivalence. They participate in the unity and coherence of Lowell's work at the same time that they show the range of his style.

Except for the ambiguous accents of "Our Fathers," a clear pattern of strenuous iambs marches through the opening line of "Children of Light," but gives a shudder in the third foot of line two:

> Our fathers wrung their bread from stocks and stones
> And fenced their gardens with the Redman's bones:

where the spoken line breaks the iambic pattern. Three slack syllables are trying to pile three stresses on the "Redman's bones"—while the imagery of atrocity negates, dashes the expectations of the phrases "Children of Light," "Our fathers," and "fenced their gardens." The spoken rhythm disrupts the iambic norm to similar effect again, notably in lines three, four, and eight (lines three and eight also break, symmetrically, the scheme of strong rhymed couplets), and the whole poem is a rip tide of conflicts: the reverend Pilgrim Fathers were "unhouseled by Geneva's night," dispossessed and cut off from the sacrament of the Eucharist by the falsity, the darkness of their Calvinist protest; they embarked from the underworld, the infernal "Nether Land" of Holland; they planted in New England not renewal but destruction, "The Serpent's seeds of light"—Lucifer, dragon's teeth; and colonial New England harbors now the searchlights of modern war (and the land of plenty is a place of scorched earth or the burning of "surplus" wheat), and her houses, instead of sheltering,

6. Robert Lowell, in the symposium "On Robert Lowell's 'Skunk Hour,'" in Anthony Ostroff (ed.), *The Contemporary Poet as Artist and Critic: Eight Symposia* (Boston: Little, Brown & Company, 1964), pp. 108–9.

juxtapose rock and glass, riotous glass (having renounced the rock of St. Peter, and travestied Plymouth Rock); the candles gutter (flicker and go down the drain), the altar is empty, everything is negation, frustration, denial, and the "light" of the "children" is global violence, the resinous heart of Cain, burning and destroying what ought to nourish or create:

> Our fathers wrung their bread from stocks and stones
> And fenced their gardens with the Redman's bones;
> Embarking from the Nether Land of Holland,
> Pilgrims unhoused by Geneva's night,
> They planted here the Serpent's seeds of light;
> And here the pivoting searchlights probe to shock
> The riotous glass houses built on rock,
> And candles gutter by an empty altar,
> And light is where the landless blood of Cain
> Is burning, burning the unburied grain (LWC).

The theme is fathers and sons: the voice of the son, child of the Pilgrim Fathers, denounces in anguish the work of the "Children of Light," the Fathers' despoiling of innocence. The clash of opposites, textural as we have seen, becomes also the structural dynamic, the movement between the poem's two halves—between past and present, or fathers and sons. But who is now the monster—parent or child? The child has incorporated the father, and curses himself even as he curses Cain.[7]

The rage, however, may be felt to be excessively strident. Just when the second half of the poem should incorporate the

7. This is in substantial agreement with the reading of Hugh B. Staples, who remarks on the relationship between the poem's two halves: ". . . As in many of Donne's poems, 'Children of Light' is constructed upon a central paradox. The first five lines sum up the past; they represent the pious but misguided Puritan fathers whose material hardships in the Bay Colony are paralleled by the more important failure of false doctrine to provide spiritual nourishment: they are the 'Pilgrims unhoused by Geneva's night.' The second five lines juxtapose the present, in which the crime of Cain committed by the Puritans against the Indians has become enormously magnified into the holcaust of World War II. Ironically, the force of the Founding Fathers' religious zeal has been reduced to vain and illusory ritual. The single-minded pursuit of Mammon has vitiated piety; abundance has become excess and the surplus wheat cannot be consumed." Staples, *Robert Lowell*, pp. 28–29.

first half, and a self-condemning son comprehend the sins of the fathers, reciprocity falters. The emergent self-involvement of the speaker in his subject fails to complete itself, fails to engage the problem with its full comprehension. The anonymity of his rhetoric inhibits the structural movement of the poem.

It is still a good poem. But if it could be better, then two reasons may be given for its partial failure. The first is what Yeats told us in the year of Lowell's birth: that poetry emerges from the quarrel with ourselves, rhetoric from the quarrel with others. The second, which is really an elaboration of the first, has been given by R. P. Blackmur, in his review of the early volume, *Land of Unlikeness*:

> . . . It is as if he demanded to know (to judge, to master) both the substance apart from the form with which he handles it and the form apart from the substance handled in order to set them fighting. . . . Lowell is distraught about religion; he does not seem to have decided whether his Roman Catholic belief is the form of a force or the sentiment of a form. The result seems to be that in dealing with men his faith compels him to be fractiously vindictive, and in dealing with faith his experience of men compels him to be nearly blasphemous. By contrast, Dante loved his living Florence and the Florence to come and loved much that he was compelled to envisage in hell, and he wrote throughout in loving meters. In Lowell's *Land of Unlikeness* there is nothing loved unless it be its repellence; and there is not a loving meter in the book. What is thought of as Boston in him fights with what is thought of as Catholic; and the fight produces not a tension but a gritting. It is not the violence, the rage, the denial of this world that grits, but the failure of these to find *in* verse a tension of necessity; necessity has, when recognized, the quality of conflict accepted, not hated.[8]

The unification of meter and substance, and of the speaking subject with the object of his conscious rage, the land itself, is accomplished more fully, and as if by Blackmur's prescription, in "The Mouth of the Hudson." Whereas "Children of Light" works a traditional cross-ruff between the spoken line and the

8. R. P. Blackmur, "Notes on Seven Poets," in *Form and Value in Modern Poetry* (New York: Doubleday & Company [Anchor Books], 1952), p. 335.

metrical norm, there is no metrical norm in "The Mouth of the Hudson." Whatever transpires between the sound and the sense is organic, inseparable, heuristic rather than known. Harvey Gross declares: " 'The Mouth of the Hudson' shows no trace of either syllable-stress meter or strong-stressing. It moves with an almost deathly stillness, sustained by a quiet activity of verbs and a tragic inwardness. The poem describes a romantically sentient urban landscape—a landscape which is a state of mind and a state of culture. Rhythm in this poem is 'the poet himself': he observes and at the same time inhabits his subject, 'in the sulphur-yellow sun / of the unforgivable landscape.' "[9]

"The Mouth of the Hudson" clearly illustrates the change that has come over Lowell's style. But the poem still moves, as it must, according to the dynamics of contrast; moves just as "Children of Light" does, only better.

Stated thematically, this observation points to the conflict between fathers and sons. "Children of Light" and "The Mouth of the Hudson" both involve a movement of outrage, rage over innocence violated, rage over the crime of the fathers. To the traditional ear, there is a loss of energy with the loss of rhetoric and metrical drive, in the latter poem; but the loss is deliberate. There is in its place a new, more subtle and for its time more essential energy in "The Mouth of the Hudson." The new poetry locates the monster in the self, and realizes both in the land, the here and now, the universal, only opening to renewal.

> A single man stands like a bird-watcher,
> and scuffles the pepper and salt snow
> from a discarded, gray
> Westinghouse Electric cable drum.
> He cannot discover America by counting
> the chains of condemned freight-trains
> from thirty states . . . . . .
> . . . .
> He has trouble with his balance.

9. Harvey Gross, *Sound and Form in Modern Poetry: A Study of Prosody from Thomas Hardy to Robert Lowell* (Ann Arbor: University of Michigan Press, 1965), p. 301.

His eyes drop,
and he drifts with the wild ice
ticking seaward down the Hudson,
like the blank sides of a jig-saw puzzle.

The ice ticks seaward like a clock.
A Negro toasts
wheat-seeds over the coke-fumes
of a punctured barrel.
Chemical air sweeps in from New Jersey,
and smells of coffee.
Across the river,
ledges of suburban factories tan
in the sulphur-yellow sun
of the unforgivable landscape. (FUD)

". . . Burning, burning the unburied grain"—"A Negro toasts / wheat-seeds over the coke fumes / of a punctured barrel." "Give us this day our daily bread, and forgive us our trespasses"—"Wheat-seeds over the coke-fumes . . . of the unforgivable landscape." Where "Our fathers wrung their bread from stocks and stones / And fenced their gardens with the Redman's bones," now the Redman is black. But more than a Negro has been added to the landscape: "he" is Lowell himself. At a reading of "The Mouth of the Hudson" and other poems, on April 22, 1968, Mr. Lowell confirmed this identification, and commented on the poetry of actual, uninvented, materials: a subject that is yourself, not an imaginary person, and a place that is actually a place. Historical solidity does not inhibit literary resonance. "A single man," isolated, he "stands like a bird-watcher," but the scene is like Avernus (ἄορνος), "without birds," a place "where birds cannot live on account of the pestilential exhalations" of the Jersey flats; "the entrance to the infernal regions; the infernal regions themselves," in Ovid.[10] The antithetical movement between the implicit expectations of "a bird-watcher" and the abominable Avernus this one watches, between the isolated man and his ambivalent integration into the landscape, makes a figure of all process and one that is elaborated by the details of the rest

10. The etymology of Avernus, and the quoted meanings, may be found in Cassell's Latin Dictionary (New York: Funk & Wagnalls, n.d.).

of the poem—and of the poet's work. The pepper and salt snow in line two, for example, has not only a prosy accuracy as a description of snow in New York, but also a similarity to "The piles / of earth and lime, / a black pile and a white pile," that make a day-night, summer-winter, life and death, Yin and Yang, iterative image in "My Last Afternoon with Uncle Devereux Winslow," which concludes: "Come winter, / Uncle Devereux would blend to the one color" (LS). By virtue of their dynamic and radical ambivalence, the poems of Robert Lowell are all one body. They cohere as if suspended in a single substance, which is also the cohesive principle of each poem. To understand this principle, or substance, Lowell's books will be considered one at a time, after an estimate of their origins in his family and education and a look at the pattern of their literary connections. Happily, the latest volume, the overtly autobiographical *Notebook*, even more completely than *Life Studies* opens the way into Lowell's life and work.

~ II. LOWELL'S BACKGROUND
AND HIS CALLING

It is more difficult to evade
That habit of wishing and to accept the structure
Of things as the structure of ideas.

WALLACE STEVENS

~ At Allen Tate's house in Tennessee, in 1937, Robert Lowell met Ford Madox Ford:

Ford was wearing a stained robin's-egg blue pajama top, reading Theocritus in Greek, and guying me about my "butterfly existence," so removed from the labors of a professional writer. I was saying something awkward, green and intense in praise of Williams, and Ford, while agreeing, managed to make me feel that I was far too provincial, genteel and puritanical to understand what I was saying. And why not? Wasn't I, as Ford assumed, the grandson or something of James Russell Lowell and the cousin of Lawrence Lowell, a young man doomed to trifle with poetry and end up as President of Harvard or ambassador to England?[1]

Lowell was twenty, and a sophomore at Harvard; but he was at the very point of turning his back on Harvard and all that Ford assumed in order to follow the vocation that has made him famous in a different way. In his own wry words: "I have stepped over these pitfalls. I have conquered my hereditary

1. Robert Lowell, "William Carlos Williams," *Hudson Review*, XIV (1961–62), 530.

13

disadvantages." But the turning point, or last straw, before his metamorphosis, may well have been the affectionate gibe of Ford Madox Ford.

Lowell had evidently consulted Ford as an oracle. Thirty years later, in his *Notebook 1967–68*, the encounter became one of the fourteen-line sections of the long poem that that volume comprised:

Ford Madox Ford

Taking in longhand Ford's dictation on Provence,
the great Prosateur swallowing his Yorkshire British,
I fishing for what he said each second sentence—
"You have no ear," he'd say, "for the Lord's prose,
Shakespeare's medium: No king, be his cause never so spotless,
will try it out with all unspotted soldiers."
I brought him my loaded and overloaded lines.
He said, "You have your butterfly existence:
half hour of work, two minutes to love, the rest boredom.
Conrad spent a day finding the mot juste; then killed it."
In time, he thought, I might live to be an artist.
"Most of them are born to fill the graveyards."
"If he fails as a writer," Ford wrote my father, "at least
he'll be Ambassador to England, or President of Harvard."

In view of the considerable influence Lowell has had in bringing poetry back to earth, it is right that his oracle should have been "the great Prosateur." Even the possible echo of "poseur" is interesting. Ford was charging Lowell with being a "butterfly" and a kind of imposter in art; Ford's own reputation accused *him* of being a kind of imposter, or social climber; Lowell was about to renounce *his* social world, and undergo a real metamorphosis, entering the profession of writing. The old prosateur and the young poet are opposite poles in the poem.

Robert Lowell was born and bred in Boston. There is a portrait of the artist as a very young man in the extraordinary, autobiographical prose sketch, "91 Revere Street," in *Life Studies;* I will not try to repeat that story here. Not entirely unlike the early part of Joyce's *Portrait,* it tells about a very observant little boy and his mother and father in a house that looked out on "an unbuttoned part of Beacon Hill."

His father was a naval officer whose life was full of disappointment, at least from the point of view of his son. "And once / nineteen, the youngest ensign in his class, / he was the 'old man' of a gunboat on the Yangtze," concludes the poem "Commander Lowell," after a spirited but devastatingly ironic sketch of his father's life. According to John Crowe Ransom, Lowell's youth "passed in a storm of difficulties with his parents. He was high-strung and headstrong; they had the social position of their families, but, not having the means to live in the style expected of them, were generally in straits, and bickering. It was a bad hurt for a boy who would have revered all his elders if they were not unworthy."[2]

His ancestors were early New England colonists, Mayflower pilgrims like Edward Winslow. Edward's son, in the words of Irvin Ehrenpreis, was "a mighty Indian killer and a governor of Plymouth Colony."[3] James Russell Lowell was Robert Lowell's great-granduncle; Amy Lowell and her brothers Percival Lowell, the astronomer, and A. Lawrence Lowell, the president of Harvard, were his distant cousins. (The famous jingle about the Lowells and Cabots of Boston was titled "On the Aristocracy of Harvard.")

His patrician, class-conscious, hierarchical background is highly relevant to his poetry; but the other two literary Lowells were not particularly his models. He was once asked at a meeting of the Modern Language Association (where he had come to give a reading) whether James Russell Lowell or Amy Lowell had influenced him in any way. He responded:

. . . Well, they were considered by my immediate Lowell family almost as disreputable as I was when I began writing. They were no support that way, except of course that's the best support. They're both creditable writers that I naturally didn't imitate, I think, and . . . well, I remember something. Let's name-drop. I was in Cambridge with T. S. Eliot about fifteen years ago, I think, and sort of stuck in traffic—we were going somewhere, and talking about this

2. John Crowe Ransom, "Robert Lowell," in Stephen Spender and Donald Hall (eds.), *The Concise Encyclopedia of English and American Poets and Poetry* (New York: Hawthorne Books, 1963), p. 191.
3. Irvin Ehrenpreis, "The Age of Lowell," in Irvin Ehrenpreis (ed.), *American Poetry* (London: Edward Arnold, 1965), p. 69.

and that of no importance—when he suddenly turned on me and said, "Don't you loathe being compared to your relatives?" I didn't know what to say to him (just as I don't know what to say to you) and I paused, and he said, "I do." He had a fine voice that deepened, and he said, "I've been reading Poe's book reviews lately, and he reviewed two of my relatives, and he wiped the floor with them." I looked with admiration. And he paused and said (and the traffic was going back and forth and we weren't advancing), "And I was *delighted!*" No, I think James Russell Lowell in his *Biglow Papers* about the Spanish [Mexican] War and the Civil War was a minor great poet, really, and a really . . . not very interesting poet the rest of the time. And Amy I can't get at all but I admire her character and admire her poetry in a way; but I don't get it really and I wish she hadn't disliked Ezra Pound so much![4]

A remark of Pound's about her is reported in "Joy," one of the sections of the *Notebook:* " 'Amy Lowell is / no skeleton to hide in your closet.' "

Another of the fourteen-line sections of the *Notebook,* the short poem "T. S. Eliot," emerged from the anecdote Lowell had told at the reading:

> Caught between two streams of traffic, in the gloom
> of Memorial Hall and Harvard's war-dead. . . . And he:
> "Don't you loathe to be compared with your relatives?
> I do. I've just found two of mine reviewed by Poe.
> He wiped the floor with them . . . and I was delighted."
> Then on with warden's pace across the Yard,
> talking of Pound, "It's balls to say he isn't
> the way he is. . . . He's better though. This year,
> he no longer wants to rebuild the Temple at Jerusalem.
> Yes, he's better. 'You speak,' he said, when he'd talked two
> hours.
> By then I had absolutely nothing to say."
> Ah, Tom, one muse, one music, had one the luck—
> lost in the dark night of the brilliant talkers,
> humor and boredom from the everlasting dross!

Its flavor of Dante's *Inferno* is just. In the first place, it suggests that Eliot is to Lowell as Vergil is to Dante. In the second place, it was in "A Talk on Dante" that Eliot spoke of

4. Transcribed from a tape recording of Robert Lowell's reading for the Modern Language Association at the Palmer House in Chicago on December 27, 1967.

the "possibility of fusion between the sordidly realistic and the phantasmagoric, the possibility of the juxtaposition of the matter of fact and the fantasic." Comparing Lowell's poem with the *Divine Comedy* might seem to overwhelm the deliberately casual, unrhymed sonnet; and yet, *mutatis mutandis*, the echo of Dante ("And he:") announces the expansion of the merely personal anecdote towards a pattern of universal significance. Lowell himself, in the "Afterthought," asks for his *Notebook* to be regarded as "one poem, jagged in pattern, but not a conglomeration or sequence of related material." Robert Lowell's verse, in the words of Gabriel Pearson (who had not yet seen the *Notebook*), "explores a condition in which public worlds have to be built and sustained out of the rubble of a purely personal existence."[5] Lowell, caught between the living and the dead—"between two streams of traffic, in the gloom / of Memorial Hall and Harvard's wardead"—finds himself at one with T. S. Eliot ("Ah Tom, one muse, one music, had one the luck—") in the project of rebuilding out of rubble—"lost in the dark night of the brilliant talkers, / humor and boredom from the everlasting dross!" But it is *words*, whether written or spoken, that offer this power; it is not an exclusively written, poetic art. "Before I made men talk and write with words," says Lowell's Prometheus, "knowledge dropped like a dry stick into the fire of their memories, fed that fading blaze an instant, then died without leaving an ash behind." Both in *Notebook 1967–68* and in Lowell's work as a whole, the anecdotal material of the poet's life and the mythic pretensions of poetry as an art are fused.

His full name is Robert Traill Spence Lowell. He is a grandson and (like his father before him) a namesake of the headmaster of St. Mark's School, which he attended. At St. Mark's he was nicknamed "Cal," after the Roman Emperor Caligula "because he was so uncouth," according to the *Time* cover story (June 2, 1967; the cover portrait is Sidney Nolan's drawing of Robert Lowell as the Emperor Caligula). "He

5. Gabriel Pearson, "Robert Lowell," *The Review*, 20 (March, 1969), 5.

liked that, and today is still known as Cal." ". . . My name-sake, not the last Caligula," Lowell calls him in a poem that appeared in *Partisan Review,* and in *For the Union Dead,* and, reduced from fifty-one to fourteen lines, in *Notebook 1967–68:* "Caligula."

> My namesake, Little Boots, Caligula,
> you disappoint me. Tell me what you saw—
> Item: your body hairy, badly made,
> head hairless, smoother than your marble head;
> Item: eyes hollow, hollow temples, red
> cheeks roughed with rouge, legs spindly, hands that leave
> a clammy snail's trail on your wilting sleeve,
> your hand no hand can hold . . . bald head, thin neck—
> you wished the Romans had a single neck.
> That was no artist's bubble. Animals
> ripened for your arenas suffered less
> than you when slaughtered—yours the lawlessness
> of something simple that has lost its law,
> my namesake, not the last Caligula.

In the *Notebook,* "Caligula" follows "Night Sweat," another self-portrait of the artist, which is also repeated from the volume *For the Union Dead.* "Night Sweat" concludes:

> one life, one writing! But the downward glide
> and bias of existing wrings us dry—
> always inside me is the child who died,
> always inside me is his will to die—
> one universe, one body . . . in this urn
> the animal night-sweats of the spirit burn.

Caligula, "my lowest depths of possibility," as Lowell calls him in *For the Union Dead,* touches bottom, the place where all the ladders start, the point of creation itself. "April's End," the sequence of which the two poems now form part, comes midway in the summer-to-summer cycle of Lowell's year, and marks the renewal of life, or creation, after "New Year's 1968." "April's End" opens with a figure of the old year made new in "King David Senex," who in his age is troubled with night-sweat (Lowell is half a century old in the year of the *Notebook*) but after an illness renews his well-known potency: ". . . later, the Monarch's well-beloved shaft / lay quaking in her haven." The sequence concludes with "Nostalgie de la Boue," where again in sweat the high and the low, the muse of poetry and the mud of protozoa, touch:

> Sometimes for days I only hear one voice,
> one shirt that lasts five days, and not for saving.
> As a child my other wife climbed a chair to dress;
> "It was easier." It's easier to miss food,
> not brush my teeth, forget to open mail;
> the Muse shouts like vacation in my ear:
> nostalgie de la boue that shelters ape
> and protozoa from the rights of man.

Cal Lowell went to Harvard, but left after his sophomore year. He did meet Robert Frost while he was in Cambridge, but Harvard did not have what he wanted and his father drove him crazy. There is a glimpse of his student life, when he was twenty, and the crisis of his rage at his father, in one of the sections of the "Charles River" sequence in the *Notebook*:

> My father's letter to your father, saying
> tersely and much too stiffly that he knew
> you'd been going to my college rooms alone—
> I can still almost crackle that slight note in my hand.
> I see your outraged father; you, his outraged daughter;
> myself brooding in fire and a dark quiet
> on the abandoned steps of the Harvard Fieldhouse,
> calming my hot nerves and enflaming my mind's
> nomad quicksilver by saying Lycidas—
> Then punctiliously handing the letter to my father.
> I knocked him down. He half-reclined on the carpet;
> Mother called from the top of the carpeted stairs—
> our glass door locking behind me, no cover; you
> idling in your station wagon, no retreat.

Time reports the sequel: "As Commander Lowell saw it, his crazed son would have to be packed off to an asylum, but family friends convinced him that his poet son needed not so much the company of keepers as that of other poets—specifically, those living in Tennessee."

But the sequel in Lowell's conscience and poetry was to have no end: "I struck my father; later my apology / hardly scratched the surface of his invisible / coronary . . . never to be effaced" (NBK). He returned to the scene of that primal crime in "Rebellion," in *Lord Weary's Castle:*

> There was rebellion, father, when the mock
> French windows slammed and you hove backward, rammed
> Into your heirlooms, screens, a glass-cased clock,
> The highboy quaking to its toes. You damned
> My arm that cast your house upon your head
> And broke the chimney flintlock on your skull.
> Last night the moon was full:
> . . . .
> . . . . O father, on my farm
> I added field to field
> And I have sealed
> An everlasting pact
> With Dives to contract
> The world that spreads in pain;
> But the world spread
> When the clubbed flintlock broke my father's brain.

In the high style of *Lord Weary's Castle*, the crime is mythologized by exaggeration; but not exorcised. It pursues him like original sin, down the years, into "Middle Age" in *For the Union Dead:*

> Now the midwinter grind
> is on me, New York
> drills through my nerves,
> as I walk
> the chewed-up streets.
>
> At forty-five,
> what next, what next?
> At every corner,
> I meet my Father,
> my age, still alive.
>
> Father, forgive me
> my injuries,
> as I forgive
> those I
> have injured!
>
> You never climbed
> Mount Sion, yet left
> dinosaur
> death-steps on the crust,
> where I must walk.

In the flattened style of *For the Union Dead* the crime is sounded again, brought low to the secular ground of the asphalt streets, yet at the same time projected into myth as the "dinosaur / death-steps on the crust" of the planet itself, "where I must walk." By the time of the "Charles River" sequence, in *Notebook 1967–68*, it is felt to be as cyclic as the "invisible / coronary" blood stream, and as the waters of the river, and as the infinite stars: ". . . if we leaned forward, and should dip a finger / into the river's momentary black flow, / the infinite small stars would break like fish."

From Harvard he went to Kenyon College, where he majored in classics and graduated *summa cum laude;* he was also Phi Beta Kappa and class valedictorian. But how he got from Harvard to Kenyon makes an interesting story. The Boston psychiatrist and sonneteer, Merrill Moore, a Tennessean and one of the Fugitive group, must have been one of the Boston friends who sent Lowell to Allen Tate—then living in a house called "Benfolly," outside of Nashville, I believe. (*Time* says a house in Monteagle, near Chattanooga.) In a vignette called "Visiting the Tates," published in *Sewanee Review* in 1959, Lowell tells how he "crashed the civilization of the South" in April, 1937, and discovered (partly from Ford Madox Ford!) that he was "Northern, disembodied, a Platonist, a puritan, an abolitionist." When he came to the Tates a second time, intent on a longer visit, the house was already filled with Ford Madox Ford and his wife and secretary. "Instantly, and with keen, idealistic, adolescent heedlessness, I offered myself as a guest. The Tates' way of refusing was to say that there was no room for me unless I pitched a tent on the lawn. A few days later, I returned with an olive Sears-Roebuck-Nashville umbrella tent. I stayed three months."

His vocation was strong. Allen Tate sent him to Kenyon, to study with John Crowe Ransom. According to Ransom: "He did more than come under our official attention: he passed beneath the lintel of my door, and lived for a year in our house. . . . Lowell was not the man, as he is not now the man, that one could hold off very long at an official distance. His animal spirits were high, his personality was spontaneous, so that he was a little bit overpowering. We had Randall Jarrell in our house too, an M.A. graduate; and if a few others came in sometimes, our tone became that of a hilarious party, and Lowell was the life of it."[6]

Peter Taylor was a roommate of Lowell's at Kenyon. The character Jim Prewitt, in Peter Taylor's story, "1939," is a barely disguised Cal Lowell. The story, about a holiday trip to New York, describes a fight between the two young writers on the train back. Lowell, in turn, has written a poem, "To Peter Taylor on the Feast of the Epiphany," in *Lord Weary's Castle*, and the unrhymed sonnet "For Peter Taylor," in *Notebook 1967–68*. The latter offers this glimpse of their life at Kenyon: "I can almost touch and smell / those pajamas we were too brush-off to change, / and wore as winter underwear through our trousers." It concludes with a touch of Lowell's characteristic ambivalence: ". . . love teases. We're one still, we are weaker, wilder— / stuck in one room again, we want to fight." "For Peter Taylor" is followed (under the heading "School") by "Randall Jarrell," a poem that concludes with a question which is echoed from the ambiguous ending of Jarrell's "Losses" but which is very close to home in Lowell's work: "But tell me, / Cal, why did we live? Why do we die?"

While he was still an undergraduate at Kenyon Lowell married the writer Jean Stafford, who was (like Jarrell) a couple of years older than Lowell and an assistant professor at another college. After his graduation they first went south, to Louisiana State University and the *Southern Review*, with which Jean Stafford was associated, and then north to Greenwich Village and the Catholic publishers Sheed & Ward, for whom Lowell worked for a year. At Kenyon this son of the Puritan Fathers had become a Roman Catholic convert.

But Lowell's Catholicism, instead of supplanting his Puritanism, has tended to counterpoint it—like the contrasting sixth section of "The Quaker Graveyard in Nantucket," "Our Lady of Walsingham." "Our Lady of Walsingham" (an adaptation, Lowell tells us in a note, of certain passages from E. I. Watkin's *Catholic Art and Culture*) makes, with its serenity,

6. John Crowe Ransom, "A Look Backwards and a Note of Hope," *Harvard Advocate*, CXLV (November, 1961), 22.

a ground, a space, a sounding board for the great violence that dominates the poem as a whole.[7] It is as if the Catholic section had been inserted into the Protestant matrix of the rest of the poem much as Lowell's brief conversion has done in the context of his life as a whole. "The Quaker Graveyard in Nantucket" further encourages such an analogy by being a hybrid of literary antecedents Catholic and Protestant. John Thompson and Marjorie Perloff find it comparable in detail with Milton's "Lycidas,"[8] while at the same time its obscurity and fiercely original style bring to mind the obscurity and syntactical violence of "The Wreck of the Deutschland," Hopkins' great poem of violent death at sea, which Lowell greatly admired in his essay, "Hopkins' Sanctity" (1944). But perhaps the hybrid is natural. Milton and Hopkins both wrote in the same way Lowell said he and Berryman had done: "John, we used the language as if we made it" (NBK).

Lowell's double allegiance in religion is matched by a double allegiance in citizenship: the tension between loyalty to country and loyalty to the world. "Every man belongs to his nation and to the world. He can only, as things are, belong to the world by belonging to his own nation. Yet the sovereign nations, despite their feverish last minute existence, are really obsolete. They imperil the lives that they were created to protect," he declared in a symposium with Hannah Arendt and others, in *Partisan Review* (Winter, 1962). That was

7. Although Hugh Staples calls it a "contrasting harmonious largo" (Hugh B. Staples, *Robert Lowell: The First Twenty Years* [New York: Farrar, Straus & Cudahy, 1962], p. 46), Marjorie Perloff feels that this section fails to integrate with the rest, so great is its contrast (Marjorie Perloff, "Death by Water: The Winslow Elegies of Robert Lowell," *English Literary History* / ELH, XXXIV [1967], 128–29). But Perloff's reading misses the point, which is not the simple one that the speaker's religion is better than his cousin's, but the ambivalent one that the whole modern world ("and the world shall come to Walsingham") comes down to the Kafkan riddle of the vacant face which, "Expressionless, expresses God." The ambivalence of the poem's conclusion, "The Lord survives the rainbow of His will," is integrated with the ambivalence of Part VI, and the poem as a whole sublates Part VI, with its terrifying silence, as a contrasting structural element.

8. *Ibid.*, p. 125, citing John Thompson, in a review of *Life Studies* in the *Kenyon Review*, XXI (1959), 485.

shortly after the experience of cold-war nuclear terror that is reflected in For the Union Dead in "Fall 1961." But even during World War II, Lowell was a conscientious objector. He had tried to serve first in the army and then in the navy but was physically unfit. (His myopia is a recurrent theme in his poetry.) Later he refused to obey the draft and was sentenced to the penitentiary for a year and a day. According to John McCormick, Lowell was sentenced as a felon because at his trial, in 1943, he "offered in defense not religious convictions or standard pacifistic volutions but arguments against the Allied, and specifically American, demand for unconditional surrender, and against saturation bombing."[9] The Time cover story gives the following account of his refusal to obey the draft:

. . . As the war went on, he changed his mind, or the war changed its character. When the draft called, he refused to report and wrote a letter to the President to explain why. He wrote not as a dissident citizen to the all-powerful President of the U.S. but haughtily as a Boston Lowell to a Hudson Valley Roosevelt: "You will understand how painful such a decision is for an American whose family traditions, like your own, have always found their fulfillment in maintaining, through responsible participation in both civil and military services, our country's freedom and honor."

"I was a fire-breathing Catholic C. O.," he wrote, in "Memories of West Street and Lepke," a poem about his fellow criminals. They included "a Negro boy with curlicues / of marijuana in his hair," and "Murder Incorporated's Czar Lepke":

> Flabby, bald, lobotomized,
> he drifted in a sheepish calm,
> where no agonizing reappraisal
> jarred his concentration on the electric chair—
> hanging like an oasis in his air
> of lost connections. . . . (LS)

Lowell's identification, in double perspective, with the viciousness and vulnerability of Czar Lepke (like the Emperor Caligula) is the poem's conclusion, bringing together, out of

9. John McCormick, "Falling Asleep Over Grillparzer: An Interview with Robert Lowell," Poetry, LXXXI (1953), 271.

their whimsical wordplay on color, the viciousness of Bioff and Brown ("wearing chocolate double-breasted suits") and the vulnerability of jaundice-yellow Abramowitz, the flyweight pacifist ("they blew their tops and beat him black and blue") and, more subtly, perhaps, the earlier image of the "Negro boy with curlicues / of marijuana in his hair," with its affinity for the lobotomized Czar Lepke's "air / of lost connections . . . ," and the curiously whimsical punning on the last word.[10]

Lowell has been in and out of mental institutions as well as jail. "Waking in the Blue" records some impressions of his fellow inmates at McLean's sanitarium, a mental hospital outside Boston which "seems to collect people of old stock," as Lowell puts it. In the lines, "There are no Mayflower / screwballs in the Catholic Church," he manages to share the perspective both of the Mayflower screwballs and of the Roman Catholic attendants. It is interesting that Lowell mentions Catholicism in the poems about both lunatic and criminal: they are all Outsiders. "The lunatic, the lover and the poet / are of imagination all compact"—Lowell's poetry, his lunacy, his felony, and his Catholicism all conspired in his revolt against the heritage of the Puritan Fathers. But he is a puritan, a father, a patriot and WASP citizen, descendant of the Mayflower, at the same time that he contrives his revolt. (The "revolting" Caligula is another facet of rebellion, as Camus' *Caligula*, with his rebellion against the human predicament, serves to emphasize.) These are the roots of the tensions that animate his poems. They reach deep inside the American conscience.

By the end of the forties he had left the Church (and its then overstimulated anticommunism), he had divorced Jean Stafford, and he had married Elizabeth Hardwick. Jean Stafford's "A Country Love Story" gives an impression of her life with her difficult husband, and her creation of an imagi-

---

10. William Bioff and George Browne (spelled in the poem "Brown") were extortion racketeers with connections among the gangsters of Chicago. As officials of a theatrical employees' union they betrayed their trust and sold "strike protection" to Hollywood movie producers. Bioff had also been convicted of pandering, literally, in an earlier case.

nary lover. The story provides imagery for a poem in Lowell's
For the Union Dead, "The Old Flame," in which he recalls his
first wife, and her imaginary lover, but with a hint of Lowell's
second wife, who wrote *The Ghostly Lover*, making a
strangely ambivalent, double presence:

> No one saw your ghostly
> imaginary lover
> stare through the window,
> and tighten
> the scarf at his throat. . . .
>
> Everything's changed for the best—
> how quivering and fierce we were,
> there snowbound together,
> simmering like wasps
> in our tent of books!
>
> Poor ghost, old love, speak
> with your old voice
> of flaming insight
> that kept us awake all night.
> In one bed and apart,
>
> we heard the plow
> groaning up hill—
> a red light, then a blue,
> as it tossed off the snow
> to the side of the road.

To Elizabeth Hardwick (presumably) he writes these lines,
in "Man and Wife," portraying himself both as a lunatic and
as a shy lover:

> All night I've held your hand,
> as if you had
> a fourth time faced the kingdom of the mad—
> its hackneyed speech, its homicidal eye—
> and dragged me home alive . . . Oh my Petite,
> clearest of all God's creatures, still all air and nerve:
> you were in your twenties, and I,
> once hand on glass
> and heart in mouth
> outdrank the Rahvs in the heat
> of Greenwich Village, fainting at your feet—
> too boiled and shy
> and poker-faced to make a pass,
> while the shrill verve
> of your invective scorched the traditional South.

The dedication of the volume *Life Studies*, in which this poem appears, is "For Elizabeth."

Elizabeth Hardwick, originally from Kentucky, was to become an editor of the *New York Review of Books*, to which she has contributed critical essays, principally on the theatre, and, in 1965, a participant's account of the Selma march led by Martin Luther King.

She is the mother of Lowell's only child, a daughter, Harriet. In "Fall 1961" Lowell worried that "a father's no shield for his child," in nuclear war. Lowell is very much the responsible father, the conservative citizen, at the same time that he refuses a presidential invitation to the White House or marches to the steps of the Pentagon to protest the Vietnam war. (His refusal to appear at a White House arts festival was reported on the front page of the *New York Times*, June 3, 1965, under headline, "Robert Lowell Rebuffs Johnson As Protest Over Foreign Policy." His participation in the October, 1967, march to the Pentagon is described in Norman Mailer's *The Armies of the Night* and in a pair of his own poems, both titled "The March," in *Notebook 1967–68*.) As he declared a few months after the time of "Fall 1961," "The sovereign nations . . . imperil the lives that they were created to protect."[11] The nation, like the father, is no longer a shield for his child; and her name is Harriet.

Harriet figures in *Life Studies* ("When / we dress her in her sky-blue corduroy, / she changes to a boy, / and floats my shaving brush / and washcloth in the flush. . . ."), *Near the Ocean* ("Blue-ribboned, blue-jeaned, named for you, / our daughter cartwheels in the blue— / may your proportion strengthen her / to live through the millennial year / Two Thousand. . . ."), and *Notebook 1967–68*, where the opening sequence is devoted to her.

The closing sequence, or all of it but the last poem, is addressed to Elizabeth Hardwick. In the very last poem, "Obit," he remembers "old wives"—"I could live such a too long time with mine"—and ends his book in a blaze of candor that embraces a composite "you": "After loving you so much,

11. Robert Lowell, in the symposium, "The Cold War and the West," *Partisan Review*, XXIX (Winter, 1962), 47.

can I forget / you for eternity, and have no other choice?"
The ambivalent "you" includes, I think, even himself, his
mythic self—"I'm for and with myself in my otherness"—in his
"Night Sweat" role as microcosm, "one universe, one body,"
and, "one life, one writing," in his role as poem:

> Obit
>
> > In the end it gets us, though the man know what he'd have:
> > old cars, old money, old undebased pre-Lyndon
> > silver, no copper rubbing through . . . old wives;
> > I could live such a too long time with mine.
> > In the end, every hypochondriac is his own prophet.
> > Before the final coming to rest, comes rest
> > of all transcendence in a mode of being, stopping
> > all becoming. I'm for and with myself in my otherness,
> > in the eternal return of earth's fairer children,
> > the lily, the rose, the sun on dusk and brick,
> > the loved, the lover, and their fear of life,
> > their unconquered flux, insensate oneness, their painful "it
> > was . . ."
> > After loving you so much, can I forget
> > you for eternity, and have no other choice?

If the question is not merely rhetorical but is a real question
that elicits more than one answer, the "other choice" is comprehended in the poem: "Before the final coming to rest,
comes rest / of all transcendence in a mode of being,
stopping / all becoming." "Before the final coming to rest" is
the still point in the poem, which is, paradoxically, a movement; the poem enjoys the very structure of being, and in its
change sublates the fact of death and of change. "I'm for and
with myself in my otherness, / in the eternal return of earth's
fairer children. . . ." Renewal, in the poetic myth of Robert
Lowell, is his life's role as a poem men read—is the recovery
of life's potential in that act. The "other choice" he has is in
their reading. Of course, if it is extracted from the poem, and
stated without ambivalence, the statement does not make
another choice, and it is no longer true to the structure of
being. But when the poem is read, it ends where it began: at
the point of choice, the one act of freedom, inside the kingdom of necessity.

~ III. Before Lord Weary's Castle:

LOWELL'S CRITICS
AND OTHER POETS

A poem needs to include a man's contradictions.

ROBERT LOWELL

~ The literary background of Robert Lowell, or of his work, includes his New England literary relatives only as a minor—though hardly unnoticeable—detail. His primary context is to be found among his teachers, critics, and friends, most of whom are also poets. Those of an older generation include John Crowe Ransom and Allen Tate, to name only the foremost; among his contemporaries, he called Randall Jarrell and Elizabeth Bishop "the two I've been closest to," and the others include Delmore Schwartz, Theodore Roethke, John Berryman, and Stanley Kunitz; among his students or followers are W. D. Snodgrass, Anne Sexton, Sylvia Plath, and Adrienne Rich.

His position in the wider stream Lowell has estimated concisely in a conversation with A. Alvarez: "I began writing in the thirties and the current I fell into was the southern group of poets—John Crowe Ransom and Allen Tate—and that was partly a continuation of Pound and Eliot and partly an attempt to make poetry much more formal than Eliot and

Pound did: to write in metres but to make the metres look hard and make them hard to write. It was the period of the famous book *Understanding Poetry*, of analysing poems to see how they're put together; there was a great emphasis on craftsmanship." (*The Review*, August, 1963.) He schooled himself in the so-called New Criticism. "My friends are critics, and most of them poet-critics," he told Seidel. "When I was twenty and learning to write, Allen Tate, Eliot, Blackmur, and Winters, and all those people were very much news. You waited for their essays and when a good critical essay came out it had the excitement of a new imaginative work." But Lowell not only studied these critics from afar; his own verse was sometimes the subject of their attention.

R. P. Blackmur is an important example. In Blackmur's analysis, quoted at length on page 9 in Chapter I above, Lowell's first book, *Land of Unlikeness*, failed "to find *in* verse a tension of necessity; necessity has, when recognized, the quality of conflict accepted, not hated." Lowell's green rage was too univocal. It was too much a quarrel with others, instead of with ourselves. Then "The Mouth of the Hudson" showed, as an example of the later poetry, how far he had evidently absorbed Blackmur's idea. Indeed, Blackmur's very words were still smarting in his mind a quarter of a century later, in the *Notebook*, when he quoted some of them in "Playing Ball with the Critic," a section dedicated to Richard Blackmur: " 'Is it a form of a force, or sentiment of a form? / His logic lacerates his vision, vision turns / his logic to zealotry.' "

Lowell's powers to absorb—his powers as a scholar—were clear even before he went to Kenyon. John Crowe Ransom says this about his learning:

. . . Today there are few poets in Lowell's generation who are so learned and so pure; perhaps none who can manage the writing of verse with Lowell's twinned flairs of grace and nobility.

When Lowell came to Kenyon, he was at least as familiar with the range of English verse as is the ordinary man at the University with a year or two of graduate studies behind him. (He could distinguish a dozen lesser poets of the Eighteenth Century School of Pope, and easily one from another; as I could not.) Therefore he studied Latin, and after three years graduated with highest honors.[1]

Of Ransom and Jarrell, Lowell said to his *Time* interviewer: "I am the sort of poet I am because of them." Jarrell he has called (in the interview with Seidel) "the most brilliant critic of my generation."[2] "From the Kingdom of Necessity," Randall Jarrell's essay-review of *Lord Weary's Castle*, is one of the most intimate insights into Lowell's work.

Elizabeth Bishop, who lives in Brazil, is the only one of the poets with whom Lowell is closely associated who is not affiliated with the universities. On the jacket of her *Complete Poems* (1969) Lowell is quoted as saying: "I am sure no living poet is as curious and observant as Miss Bishop. What cuts so deeply is that each poem is inspired by her own tone, a tone of large, grave tenderness and sorrowing amusement." The description could also fit much of his own work. The familiar criterion of tension or dynamic irresolution is reflected in the oxymoronic phrasing, "large, grave tenderness and sorrowing amusement." Lowell's volume *Imitations* is inscribed "For Elizabeth Bishop," and he says in the "Skunk Hour" symposium that his poem was modeled on her poem "The Armadillo." (At a reading at Hunter College, in 1966, Lowell read "The Armadillo," along with Jarrell's "Eighth Air Force" and Roethke's "The Meadowmouse," before he began reading his own poems. The theme they have in common, a lovable vulnerability, handled with a tone that is not quite unmixed, appears in Lowell's poems time and again—as it did that night, and not by accident, in the sequence he then read, called "Near the Ocean.") In the note prefacing *For the Union Dead,* he writes that his poem "The Scream" owes everything to Eizabeth Bishop's beautiful, calm story, "In the Village." He told Seidel, "I enjoy her poems more than anybody else's"; earlier he had explained:

1. John Crowe Ransom, "A Look Backwards and a Note of Hope," *Harvard Advocate,* CXLV (November, 1961), p. 22.

2. Robert Lowell, in an interview with Frederic Seidel, "Robert Lowell," in *Writers at Work: The Paris Review Interviews, Second Series* (New York: The Viking Press, 1963), p. 340.

. . . Any number of people are guilty of writing a complicated poem that has a certain amount of symbolism in it and really difficult meaning, a wonderful poem to teach. Then you unwind it and you feel that the intelligence, the experience, whatever goes into it, is skin-deep. In Elizabeth Bishop's "Man-Moth" a whole new world is gotten out and you don't know what will come after any one line. It's exploring. And it's as original as Kafka. She's gotten a world, not just a way of writing. She seldom writes a poem that doesn't have that exploratory quality; yet it's very firm, it's not like beat poetry, it's all controlled.[3]

Their friendship goes back to the year of *Lord Weary's Castle*, and the influence is undoubtedly reciprocal. Ashley Brown, who interviewed Elizabeth Bishop at her home in Brazil, noticed "photographs of Baudelaire, Marianne Moore, and Robert Lowell near the poet's work-table."[4]

Delmore Schwartz, like Elizabeth Bishop and Randall Jarrell, was only a few years older than Lowell. When Seidel, in his interview with Lowell, remarked that Schwartz must have been a very close friend, Lowell replied:

. . . Yes, and I think that I've never met anyone who has somehow as much seeped into me. It's a complicated personal thing to talk about. His reading was very varied, Marx and Freud and Russell, very catholic and not from a conservative position at all. He sort of grew up knowing those things and has a wonderful penetrating humorous way of talking about them. If he met T. S. Eliot his impressions of Eliot would be mixed up with his impressions of Freud and what he'd read about Eliot; all these things flowed back and forth in him. Most of my writer friends were more specialized and limited than Schwartz, most of them took against-the-grain positions which were also narrow. Schwartz was a revelation. He felt the poet who had experience was very much better than the poet with polish. Wordsworth would interest him much more than Keats—he wanted openness to direct experience. He said that if you got people talking in a poem you could do anything.[5]

"Isn't this much what you were saying about your own hopes for *Life Studies?*" continued Seidel. "Yes," said Lowell, "but

3. *Ibid.*, p. 347.
4. Ashley Brown, "An Interview with Elizabeth Bishop," *Shenandoah*, XVII (Winter, 1966), 3.
5. Seidel, "Robert Lowell," pp. 362–63.

technically I think that Delmore and I are quite different. There have been very few poets I've been able to get very much from technically. Tate has been one of the closest to me. My early poems I think grew out of my admiration for his poems."[6]

Allen Tate wrote the introduction to *Land of Unlikeness*. Lowell has worked very closely with him. "The pre-Armageddon twenties and thirties with all their peculiar fears and enthusiasms throb in Tate's poetry; imitated ad infinitum, it has never been reproduced by another hand," wrote Lowell in a knowing voice, in the piece describing his early visits to the Tates. "All the English classics, and some of the Greeks and Latins were at Tate's elbow. . . . He felt that all the culture and tradition of the East, the South and Europe stood behind Eliot, Emily Dickinson, Yeats and Rimbaud. I found myself despising the rootless appetites of middle-class meliorism."[7] At a later time he spent a whole year working with Allen Tate. Here is how he described it to Seidel:

> . . . Tate and I started to make an anthology together. It was a very interesting year I spent with Tate and his wife. He's a poet who writes in spurts, and he had about a third of a book. I was going to do a biography of Jonathan Edwards and he was going to write a novel, and our wives were going to write novels. Well, the wives just went humming away. "I've just finished three pages," they'd say at the end of the day; and their books mounted up. But ours never did, though one morning Allen wrote four pages to his novel, very brilliant. We were in a little study together separated by a screen. I was heaping up books on Jonathan Edwards and taking notes, and getting more and more numb on the subject, looking at old leather-bound volumes on freedom of the will and so on, and feeling less and less a calling. And there we stuck. And then we decided to make an anthology together. We both liked rather formal, difficult poems, and we were reading particularly the Sixteenth and Seventeenth centuries. In the evening we'd read aloud, and we started a card catalogue of what we'd make for the anthology. And then we started writing.[8]

6. *Ibid.*, p. 347.
7. Robert Lowell, "Visiting the Tates," *Sewanee Review*, LXVII (1959), 558–59.
8. Seidel, "Robert Lowell," pp. 342–43.

That was the apprenticeship; but of course it was not the beginning.

Lowell began writing as a boy at St. Mark's; but even then he had an extraordinary connection: "I had some luck in that Richard Eberhart was teaching there . . . ," he told Seidel. "I never had him in class, but I used to go to him. He'd read aloud and we'd talk, he was very pleasant that way. He'd smoke honey-scented tobacco, and read Baudelaire and Shakespeare and Hopkins—it made the thing living—and he'd read his own poems. I wrote very badly at first, but he was encouraging and enthusiastic. That probably was decisive, that there was someone there whom I admired who was engaged in writing poetry."[9] The influence of Eberhart may perhaps be characterized by four recent but representative lines:

> Style is the perfection of a point of view,
> Nowise absolute, but held in a balance of opposites
>
> So that for a moment the passage of time is stopped
> And man is enhanced in a height of harmony.

They are the opening lines of Eberhart's "Meditation Two," the poem that concludes *The Quarry* (1964). The dramatic element, the dynamics of the "balance of opposites," is the thing.

There was no Eberhart at Harvard when Lowell got there, and after two years he left Harvard for Kenyon. But while he was in Cambridge he contacted Robert Frost, who taught him about the dynamics of contrast, the dramatic element, as he relates in a conversation with Brooks and Warren.

Warren: I remember now our talk with Frost some time back. He said: "What makes a line stick in your head?" That's the whole question. Like a burr that catches on your clothes when you pass. He said, "A good line's got to be catchy. A good poem's got to be catchy." Now you want to say "catchy" is based on a dramatic element in the poem.

Lowell: I remember Frost was the first poet I ever met who told me about this. But I went to him in Cambridge when I was a freshman at Harvard and I had a huge blank verse epic on the

9. *Ibid.*, pp. 340-41.

First Crusade and took it to him all in my undecipherable pencil-writing, and he read a little of it, and said, "It goes on rather a bit, doesn't it?" And then he read me the opening of Keats's "Hyperion," the first version, and I thought all of that was sublime. It's Miltonic verse and every line was equally good and terrific and unapproachable. And Frost just passed through the opening and then came to that line about the naiad, "No stir of air was there." He said, "There it comes alive." Now that's not superficially a dramatic line, and he didn't mean the other lines were poor, but he meant that it was building up for that, and the voice tone is something I think he's just extraordinarily sensitive to.

Warren: That's what we ultimately mean by "dramatic" in poetry, isn't it? At least in lyric poetry.[10]

"What we ultimately mean by 'dramatic' in poetry . . . , at least in lyric poetry," is just that subtle a question; and it is close to the heart of the matter. It was very much in the air during Lowell's formative years. John Crowe Ransom was discussing "the dramatic characteristics of poetry," as he put it, in the second issue of Brooks and Warren's old *Southern Review* (Autumn, 1935)—the year Lowell entered Harvard and was to meet Robert Frost, or two years before he came to Kenyon: "Poems are little dramas, exhibiting actions in complete settings rather than pure or efficient actions." And again: "If a poem is not a drama proper, it may be said to be a dramatic monologue." In "Hopkins' Sanctity" (1944), Lowell calls Hopkins "substantially dramatic (*in act* according to the language of scholastic philosophy)," which is highest praise.

The summer after Ransom and Lowell went to Kenyon, and a little over a year after Lowell had visited the Tates, the *Southern Review* published "Tension in Poetry." Although it does not employ the term "dramatic," Tate's famous essay advances the exploration of "what we ultimately mean by 'dramatic' in poetry." (Warren and Tate had both, as we know, been pupils of John Crowe Ransom's at Vanderbilt.) The same year, Brooks and Warren brought out the first edition of the influential *Understanding Poetry*. That whole

10. Cleanth Brooks and Robert Penn Warren (eds.), *Conversations on the Craft of Poetry* (New York: Holt, Rinehart & Winston, 1961), p. 37.

constellation of talented writers, it is clear, had rediscovered the primacy of ambivalence; reacquired negative capability; and (simply to put it one more way) returned the study of poetry to the poem: "They point to the kind of poem that takes two opposite stands at the same time, thus negating the possibility of *meaning* in a prose sense in order that it may *mean* in a poetic sense. All this, to people interested in the human element in poetry, sounds very academic, very anti-life. But what the New Critics are saying is that poetry is about a complex state of consciousness of which ideas are one, very inadequate expression," as Robert Langbaum explains, in his essay "The Function of Criticism Once More" (1965). If the New Critics emphasized form over content—reacting against prosaic adulterations, which derived both from the political concerns of the thirties and from the reductive tendencies then prevailing in the teaching of poetry—nevertheless their aesthetic was profound, as the example of Robert Lowell tends to show. The dramatic nucleus of their theory, it would seem, has provided inexhaustible power, and has fostered the revolution in Lowell's style. It is surprising and ironic, but not really paradoxical, that the political engagement of Lowell's poetry now, since *Life Studies*, is consistent with the principles taught by *Understanding Poetry*.

This is pushing things a step beyond Lowell's own account; but I believe it very probable he would agree, if he did not happen to be speaking to another point (the contrast between formalist poetry and *l'art engagé*):

. . . I think anyone could tell that my free verse was written by someone who'd done a lot of formal verse. I began writing in the thirties and the current I fell into was the southern group of poets —John Crowe Ransom and Allen Tate. . . . It was the period of the famous book *Understanding Poetry*, of analysing poems to see how they're put together; there was a great emphasis on craftsmanship. . . . Well, that's in my blood very much, and about 1950 it was prevailing everywhere in America. There were poets trained that way, writing in the style, writing rather complicated, difficult, laboured poems, and it was getting very dry. You felt you had to get away from that at all costs. Yet still it's in one's blood. We're trained that way and I admire Tate and Ransom as much as ever.

But in England that was the period of Auden and poetry was trying to express the times, politics, psychology, economics, the war and everything that somehow wasn't very strong with us. . . .[11]

But he did not renounce the aesthetic of the New Critics; on the contrary: "I admire Tate and Ransom as much as ever." The New Criticism shaped his ideas as a poet: "The kind of poet I am was largely determined by the fact that I grew up in the heyday of the New Criticism, with Eliot's magical scrutiny of the text as a critical example," he told Stanley Kunitz.[12] The magic of the "magical scrutiny of the text" is explained by Robert Langbaum, concisely, above, and by the aesthetic of the dramatic nucleus, or lyric ambivalence, as I have observed.

Even Yvor Winters, to mention a dissonant voice important in the ferment, held an ultimately "dramatic" conception of poetry, at least according to the analysis of Wimsatt and Brooks in their *Literary Criticism: A Short History* (1957). In any case the issue was an important one, and its debate was part of Lowell's poetic formation.

Not surprisingly, but for surprising reasons, Eliot may be the most important influence of them all. For one thing, Eliot, whose *Prufrock and Other Observations*, including "Preludes," appeared (like Yeats's dialectical "Ego Dominus Tuus") in the year of Lowell's birth, had written when Lowell was eleven that "all poetry" (in the words of Wimsatt and Brooks), "even a lyric from the Greek anthology, is *dramatic*"; and he had done so in the form of a dialogue, "A Dialogue on Dramatic Poetry" (1928). The climate of opinion was evidently propitious for dialectical or dramatistic[13] aesthetics.

11. "Robert Lowell in Conversation with A. Alvarez," *The Review,* 8 (August, 1963), 38–39.

12. Stanley Kunitz, "Talk with Robert Lowell," *New York Times Book Review* (October 4, 1964), 36.

13. "Dramatistic" is the coinage of Kenneth Burke: "The titular word for our method is 'dramatism,' since it invites one to consider the matter of motives in a perspective that, being developed from the analysis of drama, treats language and thought primarily as modes of action." (Kenneth Burke, *A Grammar of Motives* [New York: Prentice-Hall, 1945], p. xxii.) Compare R. P. Blackmur, *Language as Gesture* (New York: Harcourt, Brace & Co., 1952), p. 6: "Gesture, in language, is the outward and dramatic play of

The first version of *A Vision*, Yeats's dialectical theory, had appeared in 1925; the same year saw the first American publication of I. A. Richard's earliest book, *The Foundations of Aesthetics* (1921), which concludes with a notion of dialectical or synaesthetic equilibrium: "The ultimate value of equilibrium is that it is better to be fully than partially alive."[14] Equilibrium "brings into play all our faculties." "Our interest is not canalised in one direction rather than another." This means a " 'real and active determinableness,' " in the words of Schiller; a creative indeterminacy "like the poised athlete," as Wimsatt and Brooks comment, "in readiness for any kind of action." Or like a lyric—dramatic—in Eliot's view.

For another thing—and this is what may sometimes be forgotten—Eliot was the modern master of "the way down." He had learned, from Baudelaire, "that the source of new poetry might be found in what had been regarded hitherto as the impossible, the sterile, the intractably unpoetic. That, in fact, the business of the poet was to make poetry out of the unexplored resources of the unpoetical; and that the poet, in fact, was committed by his profession to turn the unpoetical into poetry"—as he tells us in "A Talk on Dante," which was printed in the *Kenyon Review* for the spring of 1952, a year before Lowell's "Beyond the Alps," the opening poem in *Life Studies*, appeared in the same periodical. The revolutionary energy of which *Life Studies* was a center was exactly "to make poetry out of the unexplored resources of the unpoetical"—including the private, homely, or indecorous, or even the prosy minutiae of the poet's own life. I have heard it maintained that the real innovation in *Life Studies* was not so much to treat the everyday as to use the poet's own personal history as subject, *contra* Eliot's influential conception of the impersonality of poetry. But this is to take a very narrow view

inward and imagined meaning. It is that play of meaningfulness among words which is defined in their use together; gesture is that meaningfulness which is moving, in every sense of the word: what moves the words and what moves us."

14. C. K. Ogden, I. A. Richards, and James Wood, *The Foundations of Aesthetics* (New York: International Publishers, 1929 [1927]), p. 91, and *passim*.

of Eliot's idea, as well as of Lowell's poems. Eliot did not
mean that the personal should be avoided, only that it should
be transformed; and Lowell's treatment of autobiographical
material, in Pearson's words, "was not making his poetry more
personal but depersonalising his own life."[15] And in the words
of C. Day Lewis (who would not have felt that he was
contradicting Eliot), "a lyric is impersonal, not because the
poet has deliberately screened personal feelings or memories
out of it, but because he has broken *through them* to the
ground of their being, a ground which is the fruitful compost
made by numberless human experiences of like nature."[16]
Although the language is reminiscent of Jung, the idea is
perfectly consonant with "Tradition and the Individual Tal-
ent."

Life Studies channeled a flowing together of currents long
waiting to be combined. Its antecedents include, I believe, not
only the work of William Carlos Williams and Allen Ginsberg,
but also *Prufrock and Other Observations*, to mention only the
earliest of Eliot's poems. And its theory can be found in the
famous essay on "The Metaphysical Poets," whose incidentally lofty distinction between the poet and the ordinary man
may have thrown half a century of readers off the real track:
"When a poet's mind is perfectly equipped for its work, it is
constantly amalgamating disparate experience; the ordinary
man's experience is chaotic, irregular, fragmentary. The latter
falls in love, or reads Spinoza, and these two experiences have
nothing to do with each other, or with *the noise of the
typewriter or the smell of cooking*; in the mind of the poet
these experiences are always forming new wholes"[17] (italics
mine). The real track was the smell of steaks in the passage-
ways of "Preludes." But the track was lost long before that—as
explained in the theory itself. Eliot sees a decline, by the time
of the Victorian poets, in the sympathetic powers of the

15. Gabriel Pearson, "Robert Lowell," *The Review*, 20 (March, 1969),
5.

16. C. Day Lewis, *The Lyric Impulse* (Cambridge, Mass.: Harvard
University Press, 1965), p. 139.

17. T. S. Eliot, "The Metaphysical Poets" (1921), in *Selected Essays*
(London: Faber and Faber, 1958 [1951]), p. 287.

English mind: "It is something which had happened to the mind of England between the time of Donne or Lord Herbert of Cherbury and the time of Tennyson and Browning; it is the difference between the intellectual poet and the reflective poet. . . ."

"We may express the difference by the following theory," Eliot continues: "The poets of the seventeenth century, the successors of the dramatists of the sixteenth, possessed a mechanism of sensibility which could devour any kind of experience." And again: "Those who object to the 'artificiality' of Milton or Dryden sometimes tell us to 'look into our hearts and write.' But that is not looking deep enough; Racine or Donne looked into a good deal more than the heart. One must look into the cerebral cortex, the nervous system, and the digestive tracts."[18] The way down is as physical as the way down through the human intestine. The real point of Eliot's theory is anti-lofty: it is that poetry is not to be rarefied. It is that poetry, by virtue of dramatistic affinities, can "devour any kind of experience," and has to: for the seat of the soul is here, all the way down:

> I am moved by fancies that are curled
> Around these images, and cling:
> The notion of some infinitely gentle
> Infinitely suffering thing.
>
> Wipe your hand across your mouth, and laugh:
> The worlds revolve like ancient women
> Gathering fuel in vacant lots. ("Preludes")

Again I am pushing things a step beyond Mr. Lowell's own explicit account, to Stanley Kunitz, which includes Williams and excludes Eliot from the influences; but again, Lowell is making a narrower point:

. . . The poets who most directly influenced me were Allen Tate, Elizabeth Bishop and William Carlos Williams. An unlikely combination! . . . but you can see that Bishop is a sort of bridge between Tate's formalism and Williams's informal art. For sheer language Williams beats anybody. And who compares with him for aliveness and keenness of observation? I admire Pound but find it

18. *Ibid.*, p. 290.

impossible to imitate him. Nor do I know how to use Eliot or Auden—their voice is so personal. Williams can be used, partly because he is somewhat anonymous. His poems are as perfect as anybody's, but they lead one to think of the possibility of writing them in different ways—for example, putting them into rhyme.[19]

Lowell is specifying "the most direct" influences, and making a point about the specific "right voice" for each occasion—rather than about the broader project, derivable certainly from Eliot, of making poetry out of the unpoetic. Whereas Lowell's point has to do with tactics, I review also the strategic situation, which embraces the philosophy general to modern art. Looking at America in particular, Lowell writes: "Williams is part of the great breath of our literature. *Paterson* is our *Leaves of Grass*. The times have changed. A drastic experimental art is now expected and demanded. The scene is dense with the dirt and power of industrial society. Williams looks on it with exasperation, terror and a kind of love."[20] But in the broad scene, on both sides of the Atlantic, Eliot and Baudelaire[21] join Williams and Whitman; all of them explored the nitty-gritty. There has been more splitting than lumping, in this matter, and we need to restore the vital balance of opposites.

19. Kunitz, "Talk with Robert Lowell," p. 36.

20. Robert Lowell, "William Carlos Williams," *Hudson Review*, XIV (Winter, 1961), 536.

21. Irvin Ehrenpreis climaxes his valuable chapter on Lowell by comparing and contrasting Lowell and Baudelaire: "Both men have the posture of a fallen Christian. Both deal rather with the horrors of passion than with the pleasures of love, and treat death as more seductive than frightening. For both of them, art emerges from profound intellection, from labour, suffering, self-disgust. They build their best poems around complex images linked by connotation, not around arguments or events. They introduce coarse, distasteful words into a style that is rich and serious. Their poems follow circular movements, with the end touching the beginning. . . . If we place 'Le Cygne' beside 'For the Union Dead,' the two sensibilities reveal still more intimate kinship. There is the same sympathy with the wretched, the same disgust with the life that imposes wretchedness upon them, the same transformation of the city-pent poet into an emblem of the human spirit exiled from its original home. Finally, it seems important that Lowell and Baudelaire take so much of the matter of their poems from the most secret rooms of their private lives. . . ." (Irvin Ehrenpreis, "The Age of Lowell," in Irvin Ehrenpreis [ed.], *American Poetry* [London: Edward Arnold, 1965], p. 95).

When I showed these remarks to Mr. Lowell, he wrote back:

> . . . You are right not to altogether trust what I say. Emphasis confuses. Williams' imagistic poems seem now imitated to death, tho some extraordinary variation might be made. "Eliot can't be imitated," after saying that I reread Lord Weary and found it studded with Eliot. He meant much to me personally . . . more than any of the poets, maybe, tho our friendship in a way was slight, still we shared many nuances, enthusiasms and indignations —many jokes. Pound said "who will understand my jokes now he is dead." I feel the same way.[22]

Now T. S. Eliot was not as accessible geographically as the other Americans were to Lowell, but there was nevertheless a direct and important contact. Lowell's books were published by Eliot's house, Faber and Faber, in England—*Poems: 1938–1949* (1950), *Life Studies* (1959), and *Selected Poems* (1965). In 1943, Lowell wrote an enthusiastic review of Eliot's *Four Quartets*: "The experience in these poems is dramatic and brutally genuine. It is one of the very few great poems in which craftsmanship and religious depth are equal."[23] And he told Frederick Seidel of his contact with Eliot: "I may have seen him a score of times in my life, and he's always been very kind. Long before he published me he had some of my poems in his files. There's some kind of New England connection." Asked by Seidel whether Eliot had criticized his work, Lowell replied:

> . . . Just very general criticism. With the first book of mine Faber did he had a lot of little questions about punctuation, but he never said he liked this or disliked that. Then he said something about the last book *Life Studies*—"These are first-rate, I mean it" —something like that that was very understated and gratifying. I feel Eliot's less tied to form than a lot of people he's influenced, and there's a freedom of the twenties in his work that I find very sympathetic. Certainly he and Frost are the great New England poets. You hardly think of Stevens as New England, but you have to think of Eliot and Frost as deeply New England and puritanical. They're a continuation and a criticism of the tradition, and they're probably equally great poets. Frost somehow put life into a dead

22. Robert Lowell, in a letter to me dated June 13, 1967.
23. Robert Lowell, "Four Quartets," *Sewanee Review*, LI (1943), 435.

tradition. His kind of poetry must have seemed almost unpublishable, it was so strange and fresh when it was first written. But still it was old-fashioned poetry and really had nothing to do with modern writing—except that he is one of the greatest modern writers. Eliot was violently modern and unacceptable to the traditionalist. Now he's spoken of as a literary dictator, but he's handled his position with wonderful sharpness and grace, it seems to me. It's a narrow position and it's not one I hold particularly, but I think it's been held with extraordinary honesty and finish and development. Eliot has done what he said Shakespeare had done: all his poems are one poem, a form of continuity that has grown and snowballed.[24]

"Eliot has done what he said Shakespeare had done: all his poems are one poem. . . ." The feature bears emphasizing because it is a characteristic of Lowell himself. Earlier in the same interview, Lowell had remarked, "All your poems are in a sense one poem." He was speaking of his own work but also of poetry itself. Robert Frost said that "there is a sense in which all poems are the same old metaphor always"; and Robert Graves, that "there is one story and one story only." Perhaps the intuition of an objective, plenary coherence ("one universe, one body") lends a correlative inner coherence to each and all of the poems it engenders. It appears in them in the form of radical ambivalence. Shakespeare's *Antony and Cleopatra*, with its structure of alternation between the poles of Egypt and Rome, and all that the alternation serves to imply, is a magnified illustration of such ambivalence. Shakespeare, not surprisingly, makes a prime example, just as he is, for Keats, the prime possessor of negative capability. Negative capability, which Keats describes as a capacity for "being in uncertainties, mysteries, doubts, without any irritable reaching after fact and reason," is both the inner phase of outer ambivalence, and a probable locus of the "sense" in which "all your poems are . . . one poem." It emerges in words, first, as lyric ambivalence, an enchantment or flux in which opposites tend to be identical, or at least in which they tend to be equally true. It abhors the univocal. In effect, it seems to be dramatic ambivalence *in ovo*; perhaps it should be considered as emergent drama. It is in any case the dynamic of Lowell's poems, and the principle that governs their interrelation.

24. Seidel, "Robert Lowell," pp. 365–66.

~ IV. LAND OF UNLIKENESS
AND LORD WEARY'S
CASTLE

Let us condole the knight; for, lambkins, we will live.

SHAKESPEARE

~ Lowell found the title and Latin motto for his first volume, *Land of Unlikeness*, in Etienne Gilson's book, *The Mystical Theology of Saint Bernard*: "Such is the condition of those who live in the Land of Unlikeness. They are not happy there. . . . For when the soul has lost its likeness to God it is no longer like itself: *inde anima dissimilis Deo, inde dissimilis est et sibi. . . .*"[1] The religious separation of reality into nature and the supernatural, bitterly reflected by Lowell's title, had the effect of paralyzing that first volume. Blackmur has explained its failure:

. . . If Lowell, like St. Bernard whom he quotes on his title page, conceives the world only as a place of banishment, and poetry (or theology) only as a means of calling up memories of life before banishment, he has the special problem of maturing a medium, both of mind and verse, in which vision and logic combine; and it is no wonder he has gone no further. *Inde anima dissimilis deo inde dissimilis est et sibi.* His title and his motto suggest that the

1. Hugh Staples gives the quotation as the epigraph to his chapter on *Land of Unlikeness* (*Robert Lowell: The First Twenty Years* [New York: Farrar, Straus & Cudahy, 1962], p. 22).

44

problem is actual to him; the poems themselves suggest, at least to an alien mind, that he has so far been able to express only the violence of its difficulty. As it is now, logic lacerates the vision and vision turns logic to zealotry.[2]

Many of the poems in *Land of Unlikeness* fail to move the reader because they fail to move themselves off dead extremes. They are too partisan to be dramatic; they lack the sympathy to loosen their rabid judgment.

But the organization of extremes into a movement of alternation turns the trick. By the time of *Lord Weary's Castle* (which salvages from the earlier volume over a third of its poems), Lowell had learned how to construct "a dramatic dialectical internal organization," as Randall Jarrell has fully explained in his essay-review, "From the Kingdom of Necessity":

Underneath all these poems "there is one story and one story only".... The poems understand the world as a sort of conflict of opposites. In this struggle one opposite is that cake of custom in which all of us lie embedded like lungfish—the stasis or inertia of the stubborn self, the obstinate persistence in evil that is damnation. Into this realm of necessity the poems push everything that is closed, turned inward, incestuous, that blinds or binds: the Old Law, imperialism, militarism, capitalism, Calvinism, Authority, the Father, the "proper Bostonians," the rich who will "do everything for the poor except get off their backs." But struggling within this like leaven, falling to it like light, is everything that is free or open, that grows or is willing to change: here is the generosity or openness or willingness that is itself salvation; here is "accessibility to experience"; this is the realm of freedom, of the Grace that has replaced the Law, of the perfect liberator whom the poet calls Christ.

Consequently the poems can have two possible movements or organizations: they can move from what is closed to what is open, or from what is open to what is closed.[3]

"The second of these organizations," continues Jarrell, "—which corresponds to an 'unhappy ending'—is less common, though there are many good examples of it: 'The Exile's

2. R. P. Blackmur, *Form and Value in Modern Poetry* (New York: Doubleday & Company [Anchor Books], 1952), p. 336.

3. Randall Jarrell, "From the Kingdom of Necessity," *Nation*, CLIIV (January 18, 1947), reprinted in Randall Jarrell, *Poetry and the Age* (New York: Vintage Books, 1955), pp. 188–89, and p. 195.

Return,' with its menacing *Voi ch'entrate* that transforms the
exile's old home into a place where even hope must be abandoned. . . ." "The Exile's Return" opens *Lord Weary's Castle*,
and its last line, "*Voi ch'entrate*, and your life is in your hands,"
addresses not only the exile, the speaker himself, but also the
reader beginning the volume of poems.

It stands at the entrance, as a sort of invocation "Au lecteur": "you—hypocrite Reader—my double—my brother," as
Lowell himself was to render that famous line, in *Imitations*.
Baudelaire's poem opens *The Flowers of Evil*. Lowell was to
dedicate his imitation of it to his friend Stanley Kunitz, who
wrote:

> On the royal road to Thebes
> I had my luck, I met a lovely monster,
> And the story's this: I made the monster me.[4]

"Pity the monsters! / Pity the monsters!" wrote Lowell in a
later poem. "Perhaps, one always took the wrong side . . ."
(FUD). That was "Florence"; its conclusion, too, resembles
the conclusion of "The Exile's Return":

> I have seen the Gorgon.
> The erotic terror
> of her helpless, big bosomed body
> lay like slop.
> Wall-eyed, staring the despot to stone,
> her severed head swung
> like a lantern in the victor's hand. (FUD)

"Pleasant enough / *Voi ch'entrate*, and your life is in your
hands." Light on the shores of darkness, the lantern is the
severed head of the ambivalent monster, the "erotic terror,"
attractive and repulsive in alternation: "her severed head
swung." Her severed head swung, like a lantern, between the
classical poles of pity and terror.

Cut off, like the exile's return ("and your life is in your
hands"), the secret of life stares out of the head of the
Gorgon. "The devil cast out may be life," as John Berryman

4. Stanley Kunitz, "The Approach to Thebes," in *Selected Poems 1928–
1958* (Boston: Little, Brown & Company, 1958), p. 32.

wrote of his own poem "The Dispossessed," which also enacts
the theme of "The Exile's Return." "I am not going to comment in detail on the poem, which is rather complicated,"
Berryman said. "But it may be worth observing that I began
with, or at any rate worked with, both the opposite directions
the notion of dispossession points to: the miserable, *put out of
one's own*, and the relieved, saved, un-deviled, de-spelled.
The first is the more important, and the second need not be
agreeable—the devil cast out may be life."[5]

The devil, the monster, the dispossessed; the exile returning; Dante's pilgrim self and Baudelaire's reader. It is the
theme of *Land of Unlikeness* brought into its own. "And your
life is in your hands," for as you enter the poems you return to
the scene of a crime, and the crime is yours. "The Exile's
Return" touches the theme of themes; it opens not only *Lord
Weary's Castle* but all the later books as well. "The concept
reaches deep into modern agony," as Berryman concluded.

The dispossession exercising Berryman and Lowell dates
from Nietzsche. Marshall Berman, summarizing and confirm-
ing Karl Löwith's *From Hegel to Nietzsche*, traces the notion
virtually down to the threshold of Lowell's poem:

The Left Hegelians of the eighteen forties were all revolutionar-
ies, but never nihilists: each pointed, in his different direction,
toward some constructive synthesis ahead. It is only a generation
later, with Nietzsche, that the spirit finds itself in the void. Loe-
with argues, convincingly, that Nietzsche could not have belonged
to the earlier generation: for his perspective assimilates both the
full force of the Left Hegelians' critical works and the total
shipwreck of their historical hopes. They had all lived for "tomorrow," oriented toward a glorious future; he saw himself as belonging to "the day after tomorrow," to a time when faith in time was
dead. Thus his terrible madness and his more terrible lucidity
incarnates the catastrophe in the drama of the *Weltgeist's* undoing.
At first, with Goethe and Hegel, it was possible for Western man
to feel perfectly at home within the world; then the Left Hegelians
insisted that he could find his way home only by rejecting and
transcending the world; finally, since Nietzsche, Western man has

5. John Berryman, "The Dispossessed," followed by a brief comment, in
Paul Engle and Joseph Langland (eds.), *Poet's Choice* (New York: Dial
Press, 1962), p. 136.

been forced to accept the fact that he can never go home again. The house of horror which Europe became in the Spring of 1939 was built on this foundation.[6]

In Lowell's poem, the house of horror is the exile's home:

The Exile's Return

There mounts in squalls a sort of rusty mire,
Not ice, not snow, to leaguer the Hôtel
De Ville, where braced pig-iron dragons grip
The blizzard to their rigor mortis. A bell
Grumbles when the reverberations strip
The thatching from its spire,
The search-guns click and spit and split up timber
And nick the slate roofs on the Holstenwall
Where torn-up tilestones crown the victor. Fall
And winter, spring and summer, guns unlimber
And lumber . . . .
Past your gray, sorry and ancestral house
Where the dynamited walnut tree
Shadows a squat, old, wind-torn gate and cows
The Yankee commandant. You will not see

. . . .
The peg-leg and reproachful chancellor
With a forget-me-not in his button-hole
When the unseasoned liberators roll
Into the Market Square, ground arms before
The Rathaus; but already lily-stands
Burgeon the risen Rhineland, and a rough
Cathedral lifts its eye. Pleasant enough,
Voi ch'entrate, and your life is in your hands. (LWC)

"The Exile's Return" is a portrait of the artist as an American soldier. It connects, both in theme and in method, with Thomas Mann's story, "Tonio Kröger."[7] And the theme and the method are cognate.

6. Marshall Berman, "The Train of History," *Partisan Review*, XXXIII (Summer, 1966), 458–59.

7. Irvin Ehrenpreis ("The Age of Lowell," in Irvin Ehrenpreis [ed.], *American Poetry* [London: Edward Arnold, 1965], pp. 76–77) comments on this connection as follows: "To suggest the aspect of the neglected artist, Lowell crowds the poem with allusions to Mann's Tonio Kröger, who stood 'between two worlds' without feeling at home among either the bourgeoisie or the artists. To suggest the themes of heaven and hell, he has seasonal references to an infernal winter, a spring of rebirth, the 'fall' of autumn, and the entrance to Dante's hell. For the motifs of im-

The creative ambivalence is prefigured in the opening image, enacted by the words: "There mounts in squalls a sort of rusty mire, / Not ice, not snow, to leaguer the Hôtel. . . ." What mounts? Squalls descend. The mire? Mire is down and squalls are up but the mire is said to mount "in squalls": up and down are actively confused. "A sort of mire"; it is indeterminate. But its rusty color contrasts with the color-connotations of the rest, the squalls and ice or snow. "Not ice, not snow," not hard, nor soft, but a confusion of those opposite qualities. It "leaguers" the town hall—makes insecure the center of security. The very phrase, "Hôtel / De Ville," reverses expectations. It seems to promise shelter, with the word "Hôtel"—until the phrase is completed, in the next line. And the French of the phrase contrasts with the German of the town.

And so on. Even the title, "The Exile's Return," acts as an oxymoron in this field.

The poem's opening images echo the opening of Mann's story, where their ambivalence prefigures the story's movement. "The winter sun, poor ghost of itself, hung milky and wan behind layers of cloud above the huddled roofs of the town. In the gabled streets it was wet and there came in gusts a sort of soft hail, not ice, not snow."[8] From the "winter sun"

---

prisonment and release he used the jail-like hôtel-de-ville, a Yankee 'commandant' and a parcel of 'liberators' who are as yet innocent or 'unseasoned.'" Glauco Cambon (*The Inclusive Flame: Studies in American Poetry* [Bloomington: Indiana University Press, 1963], p. 226), on the other hand, cites Malcolm Cowley instead of Thomas Mann: "His [Lowell's] 'Exile's Return,' counterpointing Malcolm Cowley's book by the same title, shows Europe as a shell-torn battlefield, where, despite the presence of 'lily-stands' in the Rhineland and of a 'rough cathedral,' death lurks; a brief quotation from Dante's *Inferno* lines in Canto III ('lasciate ogni speranza o voi ch'entrate') warns us that these towns are a hellgate." Richard Fein (who cites Mann) adds, "And if Dante had ever been able to return to Florence, his fate probably would not have been very different from that of the half despair that confronts the German exile. The measured hope is stated, and the exile must go through his ascent. The possibilities of rebirth, though grim, are present." (Richard Fein, "Mary and Bellona: The War Poetry of Robert Lowell," *Southern Review*, I, New Series [October, 1965], 834.)

8. Thomas Mann, "Tonio Kröger," *Stories of Three Decades*, trans. H. T. Lowe-Porter (New York: Alfred A. Knopf, 1951 [1936]), p. 85.

to the "soft hail" the essential opposites collide. And Mann's title, too—the protagonist's incongruous name—is an epitome of the story's vacillation: "Tonio Kröger." "Tonio" is all Romance, like his beautiful black-haired mother, who came "from some place far down on the map" and played the piano and the mandolin.[9] "Kröger" is *echt-deutsch* Apollonian, his consul father's rigor, the opposite of all that is feminine, or sensuous, or Dionysian.

The poem echoes the opposites contrapuntally. "The peg-leg and reproachful chancellor / With a forget-me-not in his button-hole" resembles Consul Kröger. Tonio, budding delinquent, "was in the habit of bringing home pitifully poor reports, which troubled and angered his father, a tall, fastidiously dressed man, with thoughtful blue eyes, and always a wild flower in his buttonhole."[10] Contrasting with the father-figure, "the dynamited walnut tree" ("past your gray, sorry and ancestral house") touches the antithetical motif of the story. The tree is associated with the passionate, the musical, the Dionysian side of Tonio Kröger's childhood, as Mann relates with complicated irony:

The truth was, Tonio loved Hans Hansen, and had already suffered much on his account. He who loves the more is the inferior and must suffer; in this hard and simple fact his fourteen-year-old soul had already been instructed by life. . . . Being what he was, he found this knowledge far more important and far more interesting than the sort they made him learn in school; yes, during his lesson hours in the vaulted Gothic classrooms he was mainly occupied in feeling his way about among these intuitions and penetrating them. The process gave him the same kind of satisfaction as that he felt when he moved about in his room with his violin—for he played the violin—and made the tones, brought out as softly as ever he knew how, mingle with the splashing of the fountain that leaped and danced down there in the garden beneath the branches of the old walnut tree.

The fountain, the old walnut tree, his fiddle, and away in the distance the North Sea, within sound of whose summer murmurings he spent his holidays—these were the things he loved, within

9. *Ibid.*, pp. 87–88.
10. *Ibid.*, p. 87.

these he enfolded his spirit, among these things, his inner life took its course.[11]

The whole heritage of childhood turns to sand for the returning men. "The Exile's Return" fables again the disappointment, dispossession, disinheritance a man finds when he tries to recover the lost promises of childhood. Tonio Kröger, always an utter outcast from life's feast, yet always too deeply the artist to renounce life utterly, tries to go home again as a grown man and finds himself mistaken for a criminal. He is almost, like Joseph K., arrested. The artist's alienation is figured as this taint of something criminal.

Lowell, too, is criminal—a felon, to be exact—both in the literal and in the figurative sense. John McCormick tells us that Lowell points it out; and McCormick agrees that "The Exile's Return" is its poem:

. . . By 1943 his constitutional docility had become a militant pacifism of an unorthodox nature; he was tried in New York City in 1943 and offered in defense not religious convictions or standard pacifistic volutions but arguments against the Allied, and specifically American, demand for unconditional surrender, and against saturation bombing. His sentence was a year and a day (making it a felony, he points out) in the penitentiary at Danbury, Connecticut. . . . His poem *The Exile's Return*, as I read it, was worth the felony: *Voi ch'entrate*, and your life is in your hands.[12]

The exile returning is therefore Lowell himself—along with Tonio Kröger, Thomas Mann, and Western Europe. Lowell's private felony and the Fall of Man, with Europe's house of horror in between, are each the subject of this initial poem.

"The Exile's Return," by virtue of its inexhaustible vacillation, is better than "Children of Light." In the former evil is comprehended dialectically.

"Children of Light" is topical enough. In the 1960's, for example, the wastefulness and sterility that had been envisioned in the early poem were re-enacted in Vietnam, in the willful

11. *Ibid.*, pp. 86–87.
12. John McCormick, "Falling Asleep over Grillparzer: An Interview with Robert Lowell," *Poetry*, LXXXI (1953), 271.

destruction of crops by American men, whose progress consisted in using chemicals to do the burning. But "Children of Light" is univocal in its outrage, compared to the complex voice of "The Exile's Return." The difference is in the involvement of the speaker. Outrage can become dialectical only when it is no longer exclusively concerned with loathing. The loathsome element must be comprehended. R. G. Collingwood explains it in *The Idea of History:*

> . . . This understanding of the system we set out to supersede is a thing which we must retain throughout the work of superseding it, as a knowledge of the past conditioning our creation of the future. It may be impossible to do this; our hatred of the thing we are destroying may prevent us from understanding it; and we may love it so much that we cannot destroy it unless we are blinded by such hatred. But if that is so, there will once more, as so often in the past, be change but no progress; we shall have lost our hold on one group of problems in our anxiety to solve the next. And we ought by now to realize that no kindly law of nature will save us from the fruits of our ignorance.[13]

As Jarrell, and McCormick after him, evidently felt, "The Exile's Return" is focused in the last line. The line is inexplicably translucent. It brings about a certain change of tone, after the modulation of "Pleasant enough," from the implicit nostalgia emergent in the poem's latter half, to a kind of sardonic acceptance of the human predicament. The menace Jarrell mentioned is the dominant tone throughout the poem; but "struggling within it like leaven, falling to it like light," is something free of the menace—a nonchalance. (Contrast the solemn finale of "Children of Light.") The candor here is wryly astringent to the nostalgia, while it counters the strenuous exertion of the poem's first half. The total effect feels like a resolution; but nothing is static. The line vacillates on. *The poem's contrasts are comprehended in it.*

The exile returning is, in Robert Lowell, a descendant of the exiles ("unhoused") in "Children of Light." The "landless

13. R. G. Collingwood, *The Idea of History* (London: Oxford University Press, 1946), p. 334.

blood of Cain" (which "is burning, burning the unburied grain" at the end of that poem) has spread throughout the world of Lord Weary's Castle. "Rebellion," the poem that follows "Children of Light," concludes this way: "But the world spread / When the clubbed flintlock broke my father's brain." (Lowell actually did knock his father to the floor, as he relates in the "Charles River" sequence in the Notebook.) Betrayal and bloodshed everywhere mark the human predicament with the brand of Cain, and that is what the title of the book reflects.

"My title comes from an old ballad," Lowell notes:

> "It's Lambkin was a mason good
> As ever built wi' stane:
> He built Lord Wearie's castle
> But payment gat he nane. . . ." (LWC)

John Berryman summarizes the implications of the story:

The precise cause of Cain's ruin has been lost, but the cause of Lord Weary's—the title comes from the ballad of Lamkin—is known: when his castle was finished he refused payment to his mason Lamkin and sailed away, whereupon Lamkin, helped by the false nurse, broke into the castle and destroyed his wife and babe. Lord Weary's castle is a house of ingratitude, failure of obligation, crime and punishment. Possibly Cain did not bring enough of his first-fruits, or brought them grudgingly; "I canna pay you, Lamkin / Unless I sell my land," which he will not do. Later as the stabbed babe cries in death, Lamkin calls up to its mother, "He winna still, lady, / For a' his father's land"; and the wandering blood of Cain cannot repent.[14]

The name Lambkin itself (especially as Lowell spells it) is significantly ambivalent. It suggests both lamb and Cain, total opposites: the murderous Cain and the merciful Lamb of God. Ironically, the very syllable that poses the problem of Cain suggests also, in a term of endearment, the diminutive of lamb: lambkin. And the lamb alone has ancient, numinous ambivalence: holy dread and fascination come together, wrath and

14. John Berryman, "Lowell, Thomas & Co.," Partisan Review, XIV (January–February, 1947), 76.

mercy, in the tradition of the terrible Lamb of God—as Rudolf
Otto explains,[15] and as *Lord Weary's Castle* bears out:

> *You could cut the brackish winds with a knife*
> *Here in Nantucket, and cast up the time*
> *When the Lord God formed man from the sea's slime*
> *And breathed into his face the breath of life,*
> *And blue-lung'd combers lumbered to the kill.*
> *The Lord survives the rainbow of His will.*

That is the numinous conclusion of the volume's major
poem, the justly famous "Quaker Graveyard in Nantucket,"
where the product of God's rainbow will, the blue sailors hover-
ing above the blue-lung'd combers, are "Sea-monsters, upward
angel, downward fish." "But to the girdle do the gods inherit,
beneath is all the fiends'," says Lear. Shakespeare's monsters of
the deep, Melville's whited monster, hunter and hunted alike,
God and man, are embroiled in the mindless, cannibalistic,
universal strife. Earlier in the poem,

> *Waves wallow in their wash, go out and out,*
> *Leave only the death-rattle of the crabs,*
> *The beach increasing, its enormous snout*
> *Sucking the ocean's side.*

The landscape itself is a monster.

Lord Weary's Castle is a book of lyrics in the grand manner.
By way of a lyric ambivalence that is dramatic and universal, it
engages themes as large as Milton's and Shakespeare's. At the
same time, it is an intensely personal book: the problem of evil
is brought all the way home; the monster finds his tongue in
colloquial speech.

I have pointed out the effect of the colloquial turn in the
crucial line: "Voi ch'entrate, and your life is in your hands." Its
directness is like Whitman's "Camerado, this is not a
book, / Who touches this touches a man. . . ." *Life Studies* was
to intensify the personal still further, in the development of

15. Rudolf Otto, *The Idea of the Holy: An Inquiry into the Non-
Rational Factor in the Idea of the Divine and Its Relation to the Rational,*
trans. John W. Harvey (New York: Oxford University Press, 1958
[1923]), esp. chaps. iv, v, and vi, on *mysterium tremendum* and the
element of fascination.

Lowell's autobiographical myth. But in his most characteristic early poems, he had already tapped the nucleus of the colloquial. In "Mr. Edwards and the Spider" he had discovered, in the innocent phrase "whistle on a brick," the God-awful power of simple contrast:

> *It's well*
> *If God who holds you to the pit of hell,*
> *Much as one holds a spider, will destroy,*
> *Baffle and dissipate your soul. As a small boy*
>
> *On Windsor Marsh, I saw the spider die*
> *When thrown into the bowels of fierce fire:*
> *There's no long struggle, no desire*
> *To get up on its feet and fly—*
> *It stretches out its feet*
> *And dies. This is the sinner's last retreat;*
> *Yes, and no strength exerted on the heat*
> *Then sinews the abolished will, when sick*
> *And full of burning, it will whistle on a brick.*
> (LWC)

The cheerful connotations of the word "whistle" and the innocence of diction in the phrase move against the terrifying fact of the expiration. The contrast, the irony, makes the poem.

⟶ V. LIFE STUDIES

> The artist finds new life in his art and almost sheds
> his other life.
>
> ROBERT LOWELL

⟶ The extraordinary power that can be liberated from ordinary
speech, whether in "The Mouth of the Hudson" or in "Mr.
Edwards and the Spider," shows something of the poetic potential of the whole overfamiliar, quotidian world. *Life Studies*, in
1959, was at the center of a major, revolutionary exploration of
that potential. Its movement, in the opposite direction from
that of the symbolists, belongs to the principal endeavor of the
times. O. B. Hardison, in 1963, described that endeavor as
follows: "Generally speaking, modern poets have attempted to
find a way back from the circumambient gas [of the symbolists]
to the world of the here and now. They have not asked about
the response of Man to Destiny, but about the response of this
or that particular man to this or that particular dilemma."[1] For
the epigraph to his essay, Hardison quoted Allen Tate: "It is
. . . the way of the poet, who has got to do his work with the
body of this world, whatever that body may look like to him, in
his time and place."[2] *Life Studies* studies this life.

The book is divided into four parts, the last one bearing the
specific title, "Life Studies." That part opens with the poem,

1. O. B. Hardison, Jr., "Robert Lowell: The Poet and the World's
Body," *Shenandoah*, XIV (Winter, 1963), 26.
2. *Ibid.*, p. 24.

"My Last Afternoon with Uncle Devereux Winslow." The poem's homely title suggests the recalcitrant material it is made of. "The 'Uncle Devereux,'" said Lowell to Brooks and Warren, "the first poem of the 'Life Studies' series, was four or five prose pages that I rewrote into lines."[3] Historical time and place are rigorously specified: "1922: the stone porch of my Grandfather's summer house," reads the legend. The first line is explicitly dramatic, and what follows it is entirely colloquial:

> "*I won't go with you. I want to stay with Grandpa!*"
> *That's how I threw cold water*
> *on my Mother and Father's*
> *watery martini pipe dreams at Sunday dinner.*

The tone and diction are totally disarming, but actually there is considerable compression. Pronouncing the phrase, "watery martini," for example, involves a subtly kinesthetic enactment of the flabby helplessness, the utter demoralization, of the conventions and stance of the boy's mother and father. Another example is the dramatic opening itself: the archetypal *non serviam* is latent in the boy's rebellious words.

The contrasting tones and materials of the poem are continuously dynamic:

> . . . *Fontainebleau, Mattapoisett, Puget Sound.* . . .
> *Nowhere was anywhere after a summer*
> *at my Grandfather's farm.*
> *Diamond-pointed, atheist and Norman,*
> *its alley of poplars*
> *paraded from Grandmother's rose garden*
> *to a scarey stand of virgin pine,*
> *scrubs, and paths forever pioneering.*
> *One afternoon in 1922,* . . .

(What could be less promising, as material, than the prosy line, "One afternoon in 1922"?)

> *One afternoon in 1922,*
> *I sat on the stone porch, looking through*
> *screens as black-grained as drifting coal.*
> *Tockytock, tockytock*
> *clumped our Alpine, Edwardian cuckoo clock,*

3. Cleanth Brooks and Robert Penn Warren (eds.), *Conversations on the Craft of Poetry* (New York: Holt, Rinehart & Winston, 1961), p. 41.

> slung with strangled, wooden game.
> Our farmer was cementing a root-house under the hill.
> One of my hands was cool on a pile
> of black earth, the other warm
> on a pile of lime. All about me
> were the works of my Grandfather's hands: . . .

The black grill of the screens and the boy's hands with their aleatory conjunction of black and white, life and death, become a recurrent motif; thirty lines later:

> No one had died there in my lifetime . . .
> Only Cinder, our Scottie puppy
> paralysed from gobbling toads.
> I sat mixing black earth and lime.

The powerful elasticity of the style, embracing everything, continues in the second section of the poem:

> I was five and a half.
> My formal pearl gray shorts
> had been worn for three minutes.

(Yet already the accidental gray has more than symbolic power.)

> My perfection was the Olympian
> poise of my models in the imperishable autumn
> display windows
> of Rogers Peet's boys' store below the State House
> in Boston. Distorting drops of water
> pinpricked my face in the basin's mirror.
> I was a stuffed toucan
> with a bibulous multicolored beak.

The bird and bird-watcher, aged five and a half, this only child, reappears as the man we saw in "The Mouth of the Hudson": "A single man stands like a bird-watcher, / and scuffles the pepper and salt snow / from a discarded, gray / Westinghouse Electric cable drum." A style that can reanimate these materials—not only the "discarded, gray / Westinghouse Electric cable drum," which after all has a certain Bohemian chic, but even a "Rogers Peet's boys' store"—has to be literally revolutionary. It has to "come on the scene as an anti-style," in Susan Sontag's phrase.

The poem has 152 lines. Here is its conclusion:

My Uncle was dying at twenty-nine.
"You are behaving like children,"
said my Grandfather,
when my Uncle and Aunt left their three baby daughters,
and sailed for Europe on a last honeymoon . . .
I cowered in terror.
I wasn't a child at all—
unseen and all-seeing, I was Agrippina
in the Golden House of Nero. . . .
Near me was the white measuring-door
my Grandfather had pencilled with my Uncle's heights.
In 1911, he had stopped growing at just six feet.
When I sat on the tiles,
and dug at the anchor on my sailor blouse,
Uncle Devereux stood behind me.
He was as brushed as Bayard, our riding horse.
His face was putty.
His blue coat and white trousers
grew sharper and straighter.
His coat was a blue jay's tail,
his trousers were solid cream from the top of the bottle.
He was animated, hierarchical,
like a ginger snap man in a clothes-press.
He was dying of the incurable Hodgkin's disease. . . .
My hands were warm, then cool, on the piles
of earth and lime,
a black pile and a white pile. . . .
Come winter,
Uncle Devereux would blend to the one color. (LS)

The strength of this meterless poem is hard to describe. It manages to combine bluntness with understatement. Bluntly ordinary details of the human condition acquire "something of the impersonal dignity of a natural process."

The expression is borrowed from G. S. Fraser's pamphlet on Dylan Thomas. Fraser describes a similar transmutation in "The force that through the green fuse drives the flower." "An adolescent's unsatisfied sexual desires," writes Fraser (referring to the oxymoronic "wintry fever"), acquire (in the polarizing field of the poem's action) "something of the impersonal dignity of a natural process."[4] But Thomas's poem is still in the grand manner; not so Lowell's.

Everything in Lowell's poem is realistic, yet everything turns into the animistic. The poem manages to reanimate reality. Consider, for example, the metaphoric extension of the colors of Uncle Devereux's coat and trousers: "His coat was a blue jay's tail, / his trousers were solid cream from the top of the bottle." The blue jay's tail and its balancing action suggest the bird's bright color in constant movement against the cream of the trousers. It moves as the black pile does against the white, under the boy's precociously tragic hands. The black earth is described as cool, the white lime warm—like death and life. The opposites are elemental, like yin and yang.

But the connotations make an ambivalent flux. The metaphors relate in more than one way to the underlying organization of opposites. The sky, for instance, a connotation of the bird's, is usually light and the ground underneath is dark—reversing the relationship of the coat and trousers. And the blue jay, though a proud bird, is as free as he is fierce—while Uncle Devereux, although "animated," is caught in the rigid trap of the "hierarchical."

The blue jay, furthermore, suggests that other bird: the visionary "stuffed toucan / with a bibulous multicolored beak" (in the book of the birds), hence also "Agrippina / in the Golden House of Nero" (in the later and no less extravagant description). And thereby it involves Lowell himself, boy and man, in a mixture of tenderness and terror, in empathy with his dying uncle.

And it is simply nature, the whole thing. The process that is transpiring through the death of Uncle Devereux is all life. The metaphor of the "solid cream from the top of the bottle," compounding banalities like "solid gold," "the cream of the

---

4. G. S. Fraser, *Dylan Thomas* (London: Longmans, Green & Co., 1957), p. 12. Professor Ehrenpreis makes a similar observation: "Lowell can bestow on personal recollections the dignity of history." He illustrates with the lines, "These are the tranquillized Fifties, / and I am forty," from "Memories of West Street and Lepke." (Irvin Ehrenpreis, "The Age of Lowell," in Irvin Ehrenpreis [ed.], *American Poetry* [London: Edward Arnold, 1965], p. 88.)

crop," and "top drawer," collocates their frivolity (their sterility) with a contrasting suggestion of sperm, like the cup of sour
cream in "Skunk Hour." The life force is equal to its opposite.

~~~~~~~~~~~~~~~

The fundamental contrast is simple, existential. Life moves
palpably against death. In our predicament we do not say
"with," we say "against"; we cannot see it otherwise. The poet
breaks out of the human predicament (or the conditions of
repression), and manages to get a glimpse of a different perspective; but only a glimpse. The poetry is in the predicament,
glimpsed.

I do not suggest that *Life Studies* is radically better than *Lord
Weary's Castle*, or even radically different; its materials are
revolutionarily "prosaic," that is all. A good poem in *Lord
Weary's Castle* moves according to the same principle. As Frost
says, "Every poem is an epitome of the great predicament; a
figure of the will braving alien entanglements." Every poem is a
figure that moves.

"After the Surprising Conversions," for example, which follows "Mr. Edwards and the Spider," is comparable in its movement to the dynamics of "Uncle Devereux" (although, of
course, it is less than a third as long). It moves, formally, in
couplets, and thematically, with poetic vacillation, between the
human poles of life ("a thirst / For loving shook him like a
snake") and death ("In the latter part of May / He cut his
throat"). Jonathan Edwards speaks:

>   . . . He
> Would sit and watch the wind knocking a tree
> And praise this countryside our Lord has made.
> Once when a poor man's heifer died, he laid
> A shilling on the doorsill; though a thirst
> For loving shook him like a snake, he durst
> Not entertain much hope of his estate
> In heaven. Once we saw him sitting late
> Behind his attic window by a light
> That guttered on his Bible; through that night
> He meditated terror, and he seemed
> Beyond advice or reason, for he dreamed
> That he was called to trumpet Judgment Day
> To Concord. In the latter part of May

> He cut his throat. And though the coroner
> Judged him delirious, soon a noisome stir
> Palsied our village.   (LWC)

That is the middle third of the poem (lines fifteen to thirty-one, of forty-six lines). It contains the heart; the two remaining thirds provide the body. Here are the last eight lines:

> The multitude, once unconcerned with doubt,
> Once neither callous, curious nor devout,
> Jumped at broad noon, as though some peddler groaned
> At it in its familiar twang: "My friend,
> Cut your own throat. Cut your own throat. Now! Now!"
> September twenty-second, Sir, the bough
> Cracks with the unpicked apples, and at dawn
> The small-mouth bass breaks water, gorged with spawn.

The level tone, reporting fact, the peddler's twang, at broad noon, the cut throat countering abundant life: these incongruities, their tension, this commotion of the poles moves the poem. If the middle third contains the heart of the matter, the closing lines are the intelligence of the whole. They bring the rest to focus, recapitulate the movements of the parts. A life, like Uncle Devereux's, was curtailed; that is the plot. The poetry is in the predicament, the waste, glimpsed in its movement of contrast, against the overpowering abundance:

> September twenty-second, Sir, the bough
> Cracks with the unpicked apples, and at dawn
> The small-mouth bass breaks water, gorged with spawn.

The cadence enacts the pity in its gesture. The sentence moves in an arc that mimes the life. The last line, like the season, fills with harvest—and comes down.

Fills with harvest—and its waste: as in "Children of Light." "And light is where the landless blood of Cain / Is burning, burning the unburied grain." The grain and the spawn are both seed, or the force of creation. The suicide and the burning are negation, or meaningless destruction. And so is the premature death of Uncle Devereux. If thirst for loving shook him like a snake, we are not told of it; understatement governs the later poem: " 'You are behaving like children,' / said my Grandfather, / when my Uncle and Aunt left their three baby daughters, / and sailed for Europe on a last honeymoon." The lines counterpoint sentimentality with insentience—the melodramatic potential of the honeymoon gesture, with the equally futile remark of the "stoical" Grandfather; something flourishes in the motion between them. Life was there, and then it wasn't: dark and light. "Come winter, Uncle Devereux would blend to the one color." He would pass as do the seasons. Or rather, since his death was premature, *not* as the seasons. Either way it is appalling; this is a man of flesh and bone. A black pile and a white pile . . . the one color: prose boggles to explore the poem's terrain.

The poems, however, illuminate each other. The unforgivable landscape of "The Mouth of the Hudson," for instance, involves a comparable waste, and a comparably poignant movement of life against it. The Negro toasting wheat-seeds over the coke-fumes harbors life in a place of death; and smells of coffee mingle with the chemical air from the Jersey flats. The wild ice ticking seaward down the Hudson, like the blank sides of a jigsaw puzzle, ticks like the cuckoo clock in "Uncle Devereux." The "single man" who stands like a bird-watcher and scuffles the pepper and salt snow, as we have seen, is like the bird-like only child, the young Bob Lowell, feeling the warm and the cool of the earth and the lime. (" 'I know why young Bob is an only child,' " Lowell says in the concluding poem of Part Two, "91 Revere Street," the autobiographical section of contrasting prose in *Life Studies*.) The single man and the only child are figures of isolation and human want in the land of plenty. The contrast of the potential and the denial, the tension of the fertility and the want, is the principle that governs movement throughout Lowell's work.

"Ford, / you were a kind man and you died in want" (LS). The amazing simplicity of the conclusion to the *Life Studies* "Ford Madox Ford" says everything. The feeling is in the restraint, the want of color. And here for a different example is the same movement, between the extremely colorful energy of life and its constriction, in "A Mad Negro Soldier Confined at Munich":

"We're all Americans, except the Doc,
a Kraut DP, who kneels and bathes my eye.
The boys who floored me, two black maniacs, try
to pat my hands. Rounds, Rounds! Why punch the clock?

In Munich the zoo's rubble fumes with cats;
hoydens with air-guns prowl the Koenigsplatz,
and pink the pigeons on the mustard spire.
Who but my girl-friend set the town on fire?

Cat-houses talk cold turkey to my guards:
I found my Fraulein stitching outing shirts
in the black forest of the colored wards—
lieutenants squawked like chickens in her skirts.

Her German language made my arteries harden—
I've no annuity from the pay we blew.
I chartered an aluminum canoe,
I had her six times in the English Garden.

Oh mama, mama, like a trolley-pole
sparking at contact, her electric shock—
the power-house! . . . The doctor calls our roll—
no knives, no forks. We file before the clock,

and fancy minnows, slaves of habit, shoot
like starlight through their air-conditioned bowl.
It's time for feeding. Each subnormal boot-
black heart is pulsing to its ant-egg dole."   (LS)

Mechanical clock, hierarchical lieutenants, aluminum canoe, formal English Garden, air-conditioned bowl: these details sketch the sterility of law and order against which the mad Negro's rich life moves—or to which it insanely submits, "pulsing to its ant-egg dole."

The dynamics of all these poems is elemental. Always the basic ambivalence, contrasting the human wish and the human fact, moves like the path of a ball thrown into the air:

Over non-existence arches the all-being—
thence the ball thrown almost out of bounds
stings the hand with the momentum of its drop—
body and gravity,
miraculously multiplied by its mania to return. (IMIT)

That is the close of "Pigeons," a version by Lowell of what is probably Rilke's last poem, in *Imitations*. Lowell moved it out of its regular place with the versions of Rilke, and set it at the very conclusion of his volume. Its importance is as elemental as Alpha and Omega. The rise and drop of the ball make a figure of life and death—and of every fundamental alternation. The ball "thrown almost out of bounds" enacts a sort of paradox of the fortunate fall: it gains its value, "body and gravity," by virtue of being almost lost. But its return into individuation (being caught again) is stubbornly a fall out of "the all-being." The all-being is the out of bounds. The bounds are the individuation. Value is a function of the movement between them.

This movement figures the change in Lowell's style. And it figures the interesting genesis of "Skunk Hour," for instance, which epitomizes the journey to *Life Studies*.

"Skunk Hour" grew, almost literally, from sky to earth. It did so in two senses. First, one of its sources, Lowell tells us, was "Hölderlin's 'Brod und Wein,'" particularly the moon lines:

> *Sieh! und das Schattenbild unserer Erde, der Mond,*
> *kommet geheim nun auch; die Schwärmerische, die Nacht*
> *kommt*
> *vohl mit Sternen und wohl wenig bekümmert um uns,*

and so forth. I put this in long straggling lines and then added touches of Maine scenery, till I saw I was getting nowhere."[5] Moon and stars have disappeared, but the somber "und wohl wenig bekümmert um uns" (with the shuddery grunts) was retained in mood and idea. It entered the skunks, thus bringing the literal sky down to the animal earth.

The other, and more important, descent was from the ardent intensity of the poem's latter half to the first half's low-keyed,

5. Lowell, in the symposium "On Robert Lowell's 'Skunk Hour,'" in Anthony Ostroff (ed.), *The Contemporary Poet as Artist and Critic: Eight Symposia* (Boston: Little, Brown & Company, 1964), p. 109. Lowell gives as his sources, in addition to Hölderlin, Elizabeth Bishop's "The Armadillo," which suggested the skunks, with their invulnerable vulnerability, and Annette von Droste-Hülshoff's "Am letzten Tage des Jahres." This last, perhaps, suggested the hour: "Ein Stundchen noch." Lowell quotes, "'s ist tiefe Nacht! / Ob wohl ein Auge offen noch? / In diesen Mauern rüttelt dein / Verrinnen, Zeit! Mir schaudert; doch / Es will die letzte Stunde sein / Einsam durchwacht. / / Gesehen all," commenting, "Here and elsewhere, my poem and the German poem have the same shudders and situation."

almost aimless meandering. For the beginning was written last, Lowell explains:

> . . . "Skunk Hour" was written backwards, first the last two stanzas, I think, and then the next to the last two. Anyway, there was a time when I had the last four stanzas much as they now are and nothing before them. I found the bleak personal violence repellent. All was too close, though watching the lovers was not mine, but from an anecdote about Walt Whitman in his old age. I began to feel that real poetry came, not from fierce confessions, but from something almost meaningless but imagined. I was haunted by an image of a blue china doorknob. I never used the doorknob, or knew what it meant, yet somehow it started the current of images in my opening stanzas. They were written in reverse order, and at last gave my poem an earth to stand on, and space to breathe.[6]

"And at last gave my poem an earth to stand on, and space to breathe": the means of the giving is the mode of dynamic contrast. The movement achieved is the secret of lyric ambivalence—a secret as elemental as human breath. In the finished poem the mind, moving "from what is closed to what is open" (as Jarrell has said), recovers the fine frenzy of Hölderlin's stars —in skunks, of all things: "white stripes, moonstruck eyes' red fire. . . ." The air of the skunks, now their hour has come, is "rich" with authentic life—unlike the sterile and fading affluence of the village's "hierarchic" inhabitants. But the hour of the skunks has also the brevity of Macbeth's candle, shadow, "player / That struts and frets his hour upon the stage / And then is heard no more." The stage is "our back steps":

> Nautilus Island's hermit
> heiress still lives through winter in her Spartan cottage:
> her sheep still graze above the sea.
> Her son's a bishop. Her farmer
> is first selectman in our village;
> she's in her dotage.
>
> Thirsting for
> the hierarchic privacy
> of Queen Victoria's century,
> she buys up all
> the eyesores facing her shore,
> and lets them fall.

6. *Ibid.*, pp. 109–10.

The season's ill—
we've lost our summer millionaire,
who seemed to leap from an L. L. Bean
catalogue. . . . .
. . . .
A red fox stain covers Blue Hill.

And now our fairy
decorator brightens his shop for fall;
his fishnet's filled with orange cork,
orange, his cobbler's bench and awl;
there is no money in his work,
he'd rather marry.

One dark night,
my Tudor Ford climbed the hill's skull;
I watched for love-cars. Lights turned down,
they lay together, hull to hull,
where the graveyard shelves on the town. . . .
My mind's not right.

A car radio bleats,
"Love, O careless Love. . . ." I hear
my ill-spirit sob in each blood cell,
as if my hand were at its throat. . . .
I myself am hell;
nobody's here—

only skunks, that search
in the moonlight for a bite to eat.
They march on their soles up Main Street:
white stripes, moonstruck eyes' red fire
under the chalk-dry and spar spire
of the Trinitarian Church.

I stand on top
of our back steps and breathe the rich air—
a mother skunk with her column of kittens swills
the garbage pail.
She jabs her wedge-head in a cup
of sour cream, drops her ostrich tail,
and will not scare.   (LS)

Und wohl wenig bekümmert um uns.

❧ VI. FOR THE UNION DEAD

Facilis descensus Averni . . .

VERGIL

❧ It is possible that we have been witnessing, in Lowell, what Auden calls "a return, in a more sophisticated form, to a belief in the phenomenal world as a realm of sacred analogies."[1] The lower-case "sacred" is only the beginning of the more sophisticated form; the term would have to imply, to be appropriate, a discrediting of any separation of nature from the supernatural, such as had been posited in *Land of Unlikeness*, even in its title. But if the sacred and the secular are thought of as phases of a single process, rather than as separable worlds—if we, as readers, in fact, do recover "a belief in the phenomenal world as a realm of sacred analogies," where "sacred" means the same thing as "poetic"—then Auden's terms describe the work of Lowell. For ever since he abandoned *Land of Unlikeness*—since the time of *Life Studies*, certainly, but beginning even in *Lord Weary's Castle*—Lowell's work has searched the phenomenal world, the world of "The Mouth of the Hudson," as the place not simply of prosy vigor but even of cosmic, or mythic, creation.

The propriety of literary trespassing on myth can hardly be questioned; or if it is an impropriety, it is clearly a fruitful one. The interpenetration of the sacred and the secular is necessary

1. W. H. Auden, *Secondary Worlds* (New York: Random House, 1968), p. 144.

for the life of both. This structural connection between literature and myth, and between the secular and the sacred, is
concisely explained in an essay by Geoffrey Hartman:

> . . . Myth is a necessary and precarious profanation of a "sacred
> secret." And so is literature: but now speech itself becomes vulnera-
> ble and open to violation. Poetry moves us toward a new sense of
> the profaned word. The history of literature, in its broadest aspect,
> appears to be a continual breach of levels of style (high style being
> profaned, low style elevated), or a history of metaphorical transfer-
> ence (sacred attributes being secularized, and vice-versa). Thus
> literature and myth are not mere accretions to a central mystery but
> involved in its very nature. They *penetrate* and become part of the
> structure of the sacred event. . . .[2]

Lowell's descent from the high style of *Lord Weary's Castle*,
through the dramatic but still elevated monologue, "The Mills
of the Kavanaughs," to the low style of *Life Studies* and after,
enacts a movement of the pattern Hartman describes, and
corresponds to a profanation of the sacred. The development of
Lowell's style recapitulates, by analogy, the pattern of mythic
descent, the *descensus Averni*, required for the renewal of the
seasons. The project of renewal is familiar in both myth and
poetry. With Ezra Pound,

> *Tching prayed on the mountain and*
> wrote MAKE IT NEW
> *on his bath tub,*

conflating the high and the low, the mountain and the bath
tub, the sublime and the prosaic into a thoroughly new thing.
With William Carlos Williams,

> *The descent beckons*
>   *as the ascent beckoned*
>   *Memory is a kind*
> *of accomplishment*
>   *a sort of renewal*
>   *even*
> *an initiation . . . . . .*
> *and no whiteness (lost) is so white as the memory*
> *of whiteness.*

2. Geoffrey Hartman, "Structuralism: The Anglo-American Adventure,"
Yale French Studies, 36 and 37 (October, 1966), 167–68.

This chapter and the next further explore with Lowell the paradox of renewal through descent. *Hoc opus, hic labor est.*

~~~~~~~~~~~~~~~~~~~

"For the Union Dead" is the title of a poem, as well as of the 1964 volume. The poem first appeared in *Life Studies*, the paperback edition (1960), where it followed "Skunk Hour" as the concluding poem of that volume; its title there was "Colonel Shaw and the Massachusetts' 54th." Lowell read it at the Boston Arts Festival on June 5, 1960.[3] The same year it appeared in the November *Atlantic*, under its present title. When it became the title poem of the 1964 volume, it retained the closing position, following "Night Sweat." (And Lowell once again gave it the last, or anchor, position in the Faber volume of his *Selected Poems* [1965], where it follows "Soft Wood.")

Collocations are always interesting; a poem is likely to be on speaking terms at least with its next-door neighbors. As Irvin Ehrenpreis has remarked, the opening and closing positions in Lowell's books are especially important.[4] Whatever "For the

3. The circumstances of the reading, and an explanation of the local references in the poem, may be found in Paul C. Doherty, "The Poet as Historian: 'For the Union Dead' by Robert Lowell," *Concerning Poetry*, I (Fall, 1968), 37–41.

4. Irvin Ehrenpreis ("The Age of Lowell," in Irvin Ehrenpreis [ed.], *American Poetry* [London: Edward Arnold, 1965], p. 71) describes Lowell's modus operandi as follows: "Apart from what had come out in an undergraduate magazine, the first poems he published were a pair in the *Kenyon Review*, 1939. But years went by before any successors could be seen in print, partly because the few he wrote were rejected when he sent them out. Then in 1943 about a dozen of his poems turned up in the literary quarterlies, to be followed the next year by a collection, *Land of Unlikeness*. This gathering, withholding and sudden releasing of his work is typical of the poet's method; for he labours over his poems continually and plans each collection as a sequence, the opening and closing poems in each making a distinct introduction and conclusion, and the movement between them tending from past to present, from question to resolution, from ambiguous negation to hesitant affirmative." But I cannot endorse this last formulation; its emphasis is wrong. The movement is usually toward a deeper ambivalence—more complex, more comprehensive, or more intense. The projection by Professor Ehrenpreis is incorrect. It is, for one thing, an anticlimactic order. With the possible exception of "Beyond the Alps," which is very complex (though less intense and, I believe, less comprehensive than "Skunk Hour"), the movement rises to a climax in subtlety and in scope, rather than merely to some cautiously happy ending. "From ambig-

Union Dead" and "Night Sweat" have in common—and whatever they both have to do with "Water," the opening poem of the volume—is likely to be the volume's ruling concern. Certainly the imagery of water connects the opening poem with the creative sweat in "Night Sweat" and with the destructive flood or aridity (opposite versions of the same figure) in "For the Union Dead."

"Water" is a strangely quiet poem, eight irregular quatrains in which a man remembers a time with a woman, or a girl, on the bleak coast of Maine, and the water was too cold. The images concern hard shells and soft creatures, erosion and endurance, memory and change, and some of their more intangible implications for the human lot. It opens with flat description:

It was a Maine lobster town—

each morning boatloads of hands
pushed off for granite
quarries on the islands,
and left dozens of bleak
white frame houses stuck

like oyster shells
on a hill of rock,

and below us, the sea lapped
the raw little match-stick
mazes of a weir,
where the fish for bait were trapped.

But the details resonate in the rest of the poem, when the implicit vitality of the lobsters, oysters, barnacles, and fish, cancelled against the lifeless granite quarries, empty shells, and match-stick traps, develop their intangible affinities for the

---

uous negation to hesitant affirmative" describes neither the movement from "The Park Street Cemetary" to "Leviathan" (in *Land of Unlikeness*), nor from "The Exile's Return" to "Where the Rainbow Ends" (in *Lord Weary's Castle*), nor from "The Mills of the Kavanaughs" to "Thanksgiving's Over," nor even from "Beyond the Alps" to "Skunk Hour" or "Colonel Shaw and the Massachusetts' 54th" (in *Life Studies*), nor, I think, from "The Killing of Lykaon" to "Pigeons" (in *Imitations*), and certainly not from "Water" to "For the Union Dead."

human boatloads of hands, leaving their bleak houses, the hands
of the girl, trying to pull off the barnacles, and the voice of the
poet or lover, tender but deliberately flat at the same time. It
permits one touch of color, then cancels that.

> . . . Remember? We sat on a slab of rock.
> From this distance in time,
> it seems the color
> of iris, rotting and turning purpler,
>
> but it was only
> the usual gray rock
> turning the usual green
> when drenched by the sea.
>
> The sea drenched the rock
> at our feet all day,
> and kept tearing away
> flake after flake.

The contrast between imagination's impulse to color and its
erosion against the facts at hand—an alternation between illusion and awareness—uttered in the most desultory rhythms,
catches a monotony like Sisyphus's own, yet with something of
the free, chosen, even possibly joyous endurance Camus gave
him—but all implicit, impalpable, latent, suppressed by both
necessity and choice. The poem indulges another dream, and
another wish, then flattens both against a statement of fact.

> One night you dreamed
> you were a mermaid clinging to a wharf-pile,
> and trying to pull
> off the barnacles with your hands.
>
> We wished our two souls
> might return like gulls
> to the rock. In the end,
> the water was too cold for us.

"Here poetry itself," writes Geoffrey Hartman, reviewing For
the Union Dead and referring to the volume as a whole, "by
virtue of its style—the subtler style—holds back the darkening
mind."[5] The degree of the subtle, minimal, dynamic ambiva-

5. Geoffrey H. Hartman, "The Eye of the Storm," Partisan Review,
XXXII (Spring, 1965), 279.

lence of "Water" is measured by the complexity of Professor Hartman's remark, when he observes that this poem shows Lowell "in the very act of restraining a darkening yet consolatory movement of the mind."

The water of the title becomes a figure of all flux, inhospitable to all human forms, yet at the same time the source of all life. "I often sigh still for the dark downward and vegetating kingdom / of the fish and reptile," writes Lowell in "For the Union Dead," like Prospero's Miranda, seeing into "the dark, backward and abysm of time." His mermaid, in "Water," like Eliot's mermaids in "Prufrock," half human, half fish, is a mythical conjunction of human form and animal freedom, a traditional figure of the yearning to resolve a duality that we, like the "Sea-monsters, upward angel, downward fish," in "The Quaker Graveyard," can neither resolve nor escape.

Moving from the element of water to fire, from "Water" to "The Old Flame," *For the Union Dead* progresses by coupling opposites. After the line, "the water was too cold for us," the next line is "My old flame, my wife!"—in another poem of memory, of love and separation, which concludes:

> In one bed and apart,
>
> we heard the plow
> groaning up hill—
> a red light, then a blue,
> as it tossed off the snow
> to the side of the road.

The collocation of sex and frigidity, the plow and the snow, the red light and the blue, comprehends a universe of antinomies, conjoined with irreducible ambivalence.

Such is the ambivalence inhabiting the title poem, and caught up in its new title. "For the Union Dead" salutes the Northern soldiers who died in the Civil War; but it also suggests something of a death-wish: for the union dead. "The Union," furthermore, means both the North in the Civil War and the United States now, after Hiroshima. Child of the "Children of Light," the victorious Union in "For the Union Dead" becomes a further travesty of the early promise. The final image, suggesting Shakespeare's "monsters of the deep" as G. S. Fraser has noted,[6] goes beyond the American civil rights question, or rather expands it, to drown the globe itself in a doomsday flood.

In saying this I am going beyond what G. S. Fraser said, although in the same direction; and beyond even what Lowell himself has said: "In my poem 'To the Union Dead' [sic] I lament the loss of the old Abolitionist spirit: the terrible injustice, in the past and in the present, of the American treatment of the Negro is of the greatest urgency to me as a man and as a writer." His comment on the poem was part of a letter to the *Village Voice*, in which Lowell was responding to a misrepresentation of his play, *Benito Cereno:*

> It is perfectly clear that I am horrified by the American tendency to violence when in panic, and that is what the ending of my play —the killing of the slaves and their leader on the mutinied ship— means.
> The play is set about 1803, in Jefferson's time, and the remarks so outrageously attributed to my own feelings are meant to show the ambivalence toward slavery, even in the mind of a Northerner like Captain Delano. He literally cannot see what is before his eyes because he thinks of the Negroes only as servants and primitives. But most important to me in this historical play is my lament for the decision, made both consciously and unconsciously in the United States, to have the most repressive slavery in history. A reading of Stanley Elkins' brilliant book, *Slavery*, gives a most instructive comparison between our condition and that of South America. Ruth Herschberger's notion that I am Captain Delano and wish to put down the present Negro revolt either by guns or anything else is slanderous. . . .[7]

It is perfectly clear that "For the Union Dead" belongs to that context, and is perfectly consistent with *Benito Cereno.*

6. G. S. Fraser, reviewing *For the Union Dead*, in *The New York Times Book Review* (October 4, 1964), p. 39: "The long fish-like cars suggest Shakespeare's 'monsters of the deep,' appetite preying on itself; the worst slavery is not the oppression of the Negroes but the blind appetitiveness of the indifferent whites, the obsequious conformists. Ironically, 'servility'— the word is beautifully and exactly chosen here—is traditionally a vice of lackeys, not of smolderingly indignant slaves."

7. Robert Lowell, letter to the Editor of the *Village Voice*, November 19, 1964, p. 4.

But it is equally clear that, given my context, Lowell would agree to go much further, both in the matter of the poem's ambivalence and in the matter of its scope. For Colonel Shaw has something in common with the Yankee Captain Delano, even though he finds himself abetting the "Negro Revolt" in the Civil War. Just as there is, in Lowell's words, "ambivalence towards slavery, even in the mind of a Northerner like Captain Delano," so in the mind of Colonel Shaw there is also ambivalence, as he "leads his black soldiers to death."

This ambivalence is what I will try to show. Let me emphasize at the outset, however, that the primary drift of the poem is, as Lowell has said, to "lament the loss of the old Abolitionist spirit." It is primarily an ode to the Yankee dead, a Northern counterpart to Allen Tate's "Ode to the Confederate Dead."[8] Lowell phrased it this way himself, in the conversation with Brooks and Warren: "I've always wanted to write a northern Civil War poem. And finally at 43 I did and it's about Colonel Shaw who commanded the first Negro regiment from Boston."[9] At fifty he wrote another, briefer, but comparably "northern" Civil War poem, in the fourteen-line section of the Notebook on his kinsman, "Charles Russell Lowell: 1835–1864":

> Hard to exhume him from the other Union martyrs;
> though common now, his long-short, crisping hair,
> his green mustache, the manly, foppish coat—
> more and more often he turns up as a student:

8. Jerome Mazzaro, in The Achievement of Robert Lowell: 1939–1959 (Detroit: University of Detroit Press, 1960), pp. 124–27, discusses this connection in some detail. He notes, for example, that Tate's essay, "Narcissus as Narcissus" (1938), discussing the figure of his ode, especially the question whether he should worship death, is relevant to the "solipsism or Narcissism" of Lowell's heroes and heroines. Mazzaro (p. 124) quotes Tate: " 'The question is not answered, although as a kind of romanticism it might, if answered affirmatively, provide an illusory solution to the solipsism of the man; but he cannot accept it. Nor has he been able to live in his immediate world, the fragmentary cosmos. There is no practical solution. . . . The main intention of the poem has been to state the conflict . . . as experienced form—not as a logical dilemma.' " Hence, even as a Northern counterpart to Tate's ode, "For the Union Dead" is rooted in the utmost ambivalence.

9. Lowell to Brooks and Warren in Cleanth Brooks and Robert Penn Warren (eds.), Conversations on the Craft of Poetry (New York: Holt, Rinehart & Winston, 1961), p. 45.

> twelve horses killed under him—a nabob cousin
> bred, then shipped their replacements. He had, gave . . .
>   everything
> at Cedar Creek—his men dismounted, firing
> repeating carbines; heading two vicious charges,
> the slug collapsing his bad, tubercular lung:
> fainting, bleeding, loss of voice above a whisper;
> Phil Sheridan—any captain since Joshua—shouting:
> "I'll sleep in the enemy camp tonight, or hell. . . ."
> Charles had himself strapped to the saddle . . . bound to
>   death,
> his cavalry that scorned the earth it trod on.   (NBK)

"He had, gave . . . everything" even echoes the Latin motto of
the Shaw poem (in which Lowell altered the verb from the
singular, as it appears on the monument, to the plural form that
finally embraces the unknown Negro soldiers, and all the Union
dead): "Relinquunt Omnia Servare Rem Publicam." Although
the concluding pair of lines, in "Charles Russell Lowell," invite
contradictory feelings toward Charles' heroic action of having
himself "strapped to the saddle . . . bound to death," the
primary feeling is one of rapt admiration for the Union hero.
Colonel Shaw is comparably a Union hero; but—perhaps just
for that reason—Colonel Shaw is ambivalent, contradictory,
conducive to the apocalyptic ending his poem has, when "Everywhere, / giant finned cars nose forward like fish; / a savage
servility slides by on grease."

"A poem needs to include a man's contradictions," Stanley
Kunitz quotes Lowell as saying:

> . . . In life we speak with many false voices; occasionally, if we
> are lucky, we find a true one in our poems. A poem needs to
> include a man's contradictions. One side of me, for example, is a
> conventional liberal, concerned with causes, agitated about peace
> and justice and equality, as so many people are. My other side is
> deeply conservative, wanting to get at the roots of things, wanting
> to slow down the whole modern process of mechanization and
> dehumanization, knowing that liberalism can be a form of death
> too. In the writing of a poem all our compulsions and biases should
> get in, so that finally we don't know what we mean.[10]

10. Stanley Kunitz, "Telling the Time," *Salmagundi*, I, 4 (1966–67), 22.

"What we mean" becomes, finally, the problem of the whole life work; there is no surer way to approach it than through the interrelation of the various poems.

"The ditch is nearer," in "For the Union Dead," means what the following lines mean in "Fall 1961":

> Our end drifts nearer,
> the moon lifts,
> radiant with terror.
> The state
> is a diver under a glass bell.   (FUD)

Colonel Shaw's bubble is the globe itself. As "he waits / for the blessed break," he anticipates the world's annihilation. The fragility of the glass bell, and the world bubble, is a very persistent theme for Robert Lowell. Time is running out, his poems say.

> Back and forth, back and forth
> goes the tock, tock, tock
> of the orange, bland, ambassadorial
> face of the moon
> on the grandfather clock,

to quote again from "Fall 1961" (FUD).

That poem follows "The Mouth of the Hudson," where, as we saw, "The ice ticks seaward like a clock." Like the skunks, the figure of the Negro is terribly vulnerable, terribly vital, in "The Mouth of the Hudson." It is repeated in the "bell-cheeked Negro infantry," the slaughtered infants, of "For the Union Dead"; and in their progeny the Negro schoolchildren, whose "drained faces" in the television picture-tube "rise like balloons." The bubble of Colonel Shaw, like the insolid globe itself, "waits / for the blessed break."

Apocalypse, as in James Baldwin's "The Fire Next Time," is figured again at the conclusion of *Benito Cereno* itself, third in the trilogy of plays, *The Old Glory* (1965), when the Negro leader, Babu, smashes the glass ball representing the earth:

> This is my crown.
> [Puts crown on his head. He snatches Benito's rattan cane]
> This is my rod.

[Picks up silver ball ("which is really glass"[11])]
This is the earth.
[Holds the ball out with one hand and raises the cane]
This is the arm of the angry God.
[Smashes the ball] . . . .[12]

This was the curtain speech of the play as it appeared in *Show* magazine, in 1964. Lowell added five lines in the final version, completely reversing the outcome: now the Yankee Captain Delano, raising his pistol, speaks the curtain line and shoots the Negro:

This is your future.
[Babu falls and lies still. Delano pauses, then slowly empties the five remaining barrels of his pistol into the body. Lights dim]

CURTAIN[13]

The negation is humanly total either way.

Yet this is our dilemma in real life. The world of current events is translucently the subject of *Benito Cereno*, for all its setting in 1803. As a detail of the interrelation of current history and the world of *The Old Glory*, consider the letter that Lowell wrote to the editors of the *New York Review*: "We should have a national day of mourning, or better our own day of mourning, for the people we have sent into misery, desperation—that we have sent out of life; for our own soldiers, for the pro-American Vietnamese, and for the anti-American Vietnamese, those who have fought with unequaled ferocity, and probably hopeless courage, because they preferred annihilation to the despair of an American conquest." The letter is dated February 4, 1968, a time of increased violence in the war in Vietnam. It expressed feelingly his emotions of that moment, over that particular turn of events. Yet the letter was derived verbatim—except for the substitution of the Vietnamese for American Indians—from Lowell's revision of *Endecott and the Red Cross*, the first play of the trilogy, *The Old Glory*. (Lowell was reworking the play

11. Robert Lowell, "Benito Cereno," *Show* (August, 1964), p. 96.
12. *Ibid.* Also (without the parenthesis) in Robert Lowell, "Benito Cereno," *The Old Glory* (New York: Farrar, Straus & Giroux, 1965), p. 193.
13. *Old Glory*, p. 193.

for its production in the spring.) The New York theatre and the theatre of the war in Vietnam for a moment coalesced.

Yet for Lowell they had never really been separate. Matthew Arnold could, in "Dover Beach," turn from the world outside to a private love as a separate world; Lowell can do no such thing. The two worlds have permanently coalesced. "A father's no shield / for his child." Lowell's ignorant armies seem to clash in a more intimate place; their hatred moves our stars as much as love:

> Pity the planet, all joy gone
> from this sweet volcanic cone;
> peace to our children when they fall
> in small war on the heels of small
> war—until the end of time
> to police the earth, a ghost
> orbiting forever lost
> in our monotonous sublime. (NO)[14]

That is the conclusion of "Waking Early Sunday Morning," a poem he published on the eve of the twentieth anniversary of Hiroshima. Its whimper is quite as apocalyptic as the bang. But it is also (always!) simultaneously, whatever the pain, and however negative it may be, a figure of birth. This planet, this hellish, "sweet volcanic cone," can be seen to issue as if *in parturition* "our children when they fall," in small wars like the Vietnam war. Consider the following quatrain from "The Equilibrists," by John Crowe Ransom, as a possible antecedent for the figure of "our monotonous sublime," which assumes the shape of "this sweet volcanic cone":

> In Heaven you have heard no marriage is,
> No white flesh tinder to your lecheries,
> Your male and female tissue sweetly shaped
> Sublimed away, and furious blood escaped.[15]

14. Robert Lowell, "Waking Early Sunday Morning," *New York Review of Books*, V (August 5, 1965), 3. It became the opening poem of Lowell's volume, *Near the Ocean* (New York: Farrar, Straus & Giroux, 1967), pp. 15–24.

15. John Crowe Ransom, "The Equilibrists," *Poems and Essays* (New York: Vintage Books, 1955), p. 66. It is the image connected with the word "sublimed," and not the word alone, that suggests the possible

Lowell's "sweet volcanic cone" travesties the vulva. The children fall in birth, in death, more abruptly than Jarrell's ball-turret gunner—and ironically in the stanza form of Marvell's "The Garden." The whole figure, brought to its oxymoronic close "in our monotonous sublime," joins the sublime to the ridiculous a little as Pope did, at the end of the *Dunciad*, in a comparably apocalyptic conclusion.

This inkling of Lowell's radical concern will help reveal, I think, how "For the Union Dead" is put together. The ruling ambivalence that is caught in the title, and carried home in the resonant closing image, has developed substance or traction in the body of the poem. Every detail serves to elaborate the conclusion; even the Latin motto pulls more than its weight. And governing the entire activity are meterless quatrains.

"This must be a formal poem," Lowell said to Brooks and Warren. "The parts hold together yet there's no meter. And the quatrain is, in a certain sense, an artificial one. It's sometimes kept and sometimes run on and the lines vary greatly in length; they may be three or four syllables [or] fifteen, yet I feel the quatrain is important. . . ." Warren completed the sentence: "As a minimal thing, anyway, I suppose it's something for the poet to hang on to in the process, to . . ." Lowell: "Yes. You know, just as I do, that sometimes you want something to hold on to, sometimes you want much less."[16] There the conversation ended, without explaining the mysteriously variable need. One can infer, however, a determining factor, an explanation for sometimes wanting more and sometimes less—more, for instance, in the rhymed stanzas of "Waking Early Sunday Morning"; less, in the unrhymed and even meterless quatrains of "For the Union Dead." There has to be an asymmetric

---

relevance of this passage. The actual phrase, "the monotony of the sublime," occurs in a remark of Lowell's to A. Alvarez: ". . . What everyone finds wrong with American culture is the monotony of the sublime. I've never lived anywhere else, but I feel it is extreme (and perhaps unique, even) about America, that the artist's existence becomes his art. He is re-born in it, and he hardly exists without it." (Quoted by A. Alvarez in "A Talk with Robert Lowell," *Encounter*, XXIV [February 1965], 43.) The American is a Puritan in art as in war.

16. Robert Lowell to Brooks and Warren in Brooks and Warren (eds.), *Conversations*, p. 47.

balance, a dynamic symmetry, between what is known and predictable and what is not—or between the day and night of the poem's world. Public domain and private experience are the poles of this oscillation, and so are the conscious and other-than-conscious regions of the poet's mind. Between the poles a movement is maintained. Ambivalence is the condition of that movement.

The meterless quatrians of "For the Union Dead" are themselves a kind of metrical ambivalence—neither fish nor fowl; and their ambivalence relates to the vital movement of the poem. Its proportioning of order and chaos—one infers—has to do with the comprehending affirmation or acceptance that otherwise might prove to be undiscoverable, altogether, in the rigidly arid waste land of this poem. In the words of Geoffrey Hartman's essay-review of *For the Union Dead*, the poem's movement is "the calm in the eye of the storm."[17] Its peculiar calm is further described by Lionel Trilling: "The demeanor of Robert Lowell's poem about the memorial of his kinsman is significantly unlike that of the monument itself; the salient characteristic of the poem is its air of acknowledged fatigue."[18] The flatness of manner, like the fact of death, contrasts with the memory, with the monument, and with the style of the monument's original dedication.

> *Two months after marching through Boston,*
> *half the regiment was dead;*
> *at the dedication,*
> *William James could almost hear the bronze Negroes breathe.*

Professor Trilling observes that William James had been designated the "Orator" at the dedication of the Shaw monument; his oration was elevated, eloquent, "inspiring"; its echoes (in the phrase about hearing the soldiers breathe, and, later, in the lines about the "small town New England greens" and "the abstract Union Soldier"), together with the naming of James, call attention to the contrast between the fullness of James's oration and the flatness of Lowell's chosen style—"a contrast

17. Hartman, "Eye of the Storm," p. 280.
18. Lionel Trilling, *The Experience of Literature: A Reader with Commentaries* (New York: Holt, Rinehart & Winston, 1967), p. 962.

that was surely intended."[19] In Lowell's poem the sense of order and the sense of chaos balance—as they do in the ambivalent condition of the meterless quatrains.

The Latin motto, I have said, is a telling detail. It comes from the public domain, "St. Gauden's shaking Civil War relief," as an inscription: in Lowell's version, "Relinquunt Omnia Servare Rem Publicam." To serve the public domain, or the state, a soldier gives his all; gives up his very self, his life, for the sake of the public thing, as Colonel Shaw and his Regiment have done. The poem, in its ambivalence, questions the fruits and questions the motive of the sacrifice. For the fruits are appalling: an arid, sterile waste land. The questionable motive seems thanatic. Patriotism and suicide compete—or collaborate. The horns of the dilemma are joined in the New England skull, or the abstract public thing.

The poem opens, characteristically, vacillating even in the most minute detail:

> The old South Boston Aquarium stands
> in a Sahara of snow now. Its broken windows are boarded.
> The bronze weathervane cod has lost half its scales.
> The airy tanks are dry. (FUD)

The tone is more than relaxed, it seems nearly lethargic; but inside all is ferment, everything moves, nothing will stand still. Under the Civil War title, the opening phrase manages to juxtapose Boston and the Old South: "the old South Boston." This flicker of opposition, or North-South polarity, is reinforced by the reversals in the rest of the sentence. The "Aquarium stands / in a Sahara of snow now": Aquarium and Sahara, Sahara and snow, stands and falls to ruin. "Its broken windows are boarded." Each pulsion of meaning or expectation is quickly negated or reversed: the windows—are broken; the broken windows—are boarded up. Instead of the usual weathercock a "bronze weathervane *cod*" surmounts the ruin—surmounts, or, with the giant finned cars at the poem's end, *submerges* it. Yet it is not fish, nor does its bronze endure: "it has lost half its scales." It is neither fish, flesh, nor fowl. The non-weatherproof

19. *Ibid.*

bronze no-fish swims in air instead of water, and—since everything is upside down—"The airy tanks are dry." Nothing is
what it was, everything is reversed, strange but hardly rich, a
travesty of sea-change. And yet the tone of the poem is lax,
measured by unmetered quatrains, casual, and conversational,
and dry.

The second quatrain juxtaposes to the dryness of the first a
soft nostalgia, a more lively memory of childhood (as in "My
Last Afternoon with Uncle Devereux Winslow"), with the
tanks full of water and fish, arrestingly focused:

> Once my nose crawled like a snail on the glass;
> my hand tingled
> to burst the bubbles
> drifting from the noses of the cowed, compliant fish. (FUD)

Already, between the first two quatrains, and in curious tension
with the deceptively lax tone, move those currents of nervous
life which will animate the poem—both in itself, and as a
member of the corporate body of Lowell's work.

For the internal movements are concurrent with wider affinities, which amplify them, on the analogy of sympathetic vibration. Their core opposition of life against death repeats, and is
repeated by, "Falling Asleep over the Aeneid," which Ransom
particularly admired—where the corpse of Pallas seems to say to
Aeneas, "Brother try, / O Child of Aphrodite, try to die: / To
die is life" (MK). In that poem, as explained in the headnote,
"An old man in Concord forgets to go to morning service. He
falls asleep while reading Vergil and dreams that he is Aeneas at
the funeral of Pallas, an Italian prince." He wakes, and day-
dreams of his Uncle Charles, "blue-capped and bird-like" in his
Civil War uniform, in a coffin:

> . . . And my aunt,
> Hearing his colored volunteers parade
> Through Concord, laughs, and tells her English maid
> To clip his yellow nostril hairs, and fold
> His colors on him. . . . (MK)

Colonel Shaw, in "For the Union Dead," is also bird-like, and
aristocratic, and leads his colored volunteers to die:

> He has an angry wrenlike vigilance
> a greyhound's gentle tautness;
> he seems to wince at pleasure
> and suffocate for privacy.

> He is out of bounds now. He rejoices in man's lovely,
> peculiar power to choose life and die—
> when he leads his black soldiers to death,
> he cannot bend his back. (FUD)

He rejoices in man's lovely, peculiar power to choose life and die—because to die is life. But what is the sense of this paradox, this equivocation, this ambivalence? It will not keep still. Colonel Shaw "seems to wince at pleasure, and suffocate for privacy": for the fine and private place of annihilation. Taut, unbending, Colonel Shaw has at last gone over the hill: "He is out of bounds now. He rejoices. . . ." He rejoices because, like Prufrock, he has secretly craved release into life—even though he could think of it only in the stiff terms of death. Even "when he leads his black soldiers to death, / he cannot bend his back."

But the black soldiers, the Negroes, the colored are color, are life. The whiteness of Pallas in "Falling Asleep over the Aeneid" is death, is loveliness *lost*:

> Face of snow,
> You are the flower that country girls have caught,
> A wild bee-pillaged honey-suckle brought
> To the returning bridegroom—the design
> Has not yet left it, and the petals shine;
> The earth, its mother, has, at last, no help:
> It is itself. (MK)

So the Negro toasting wheat-seeds in "The Mouth of the Hudson" is life itself; and so is the mad Negro soldier confined at Munich, in the poem by that name. When the "drained faces of Negro school-children rise like balloons" in "For the Union Dead," the seeds of life become as the "face of snow." Life moves against death, as color moves against the darkness of its absence, or of sterility.

Consider, for a complicated example, "Where the Rainbow Ends," which concludes *Lord Weary's Castle*. The title refers to the Rainbow of the Covenant, the Covenant with the Lord

Who ". . . survives the rainbow of His will" in "The Quaker Graveyard." But it also refers to "The Pepperpot, ironic rainbow" in Boston, where the rainbow ends, and where the sublime encounters the ridiculous. ("The Charles Street Bridge to Cambridge, whose towers may be thought of as 'pepperpots,' " Staples explains in a note [p. 107].) There the color absurdly promises what it does not give.

Or, for a closer example, consider the "colored volunteers" in the old man's daydream, in "Falling Asleep over the Aeneid." Like the blue of the cap, the yellow nostril hairs, and the colors of the corpse's flag, they hold life, intimate life, erotic life, over against death.

> *The sun is blue and scarlet on my page,*
> *And yuck-a, yuck-a, yuck-a, rage*
> *The yellowhammers mating. Yellow fire*
> *Blankets the captives dancing on their pyre,*
> *And the scorched lictor screams and drops his rod,*

the poem has opened—conjoining Eros and death as its governing poles. (MK)

For this conjunction, "For the Union Dead" implicitly and explicitly yearns. "I often sigh still / for the dark downward and vegetating kingdom / of the fish and reptile." The motive is persistent: to follow where all has fled, like the "wild bee-pillaged honey-suckle brought / To the returning bridegroom," and the rainbow's end. But the rainbow's end is Boston.

> *One morning last March,*
> *I pressed aginst the new barbed and galvanized*
>
> *fence on the Boston Common. Behind their cage,*
> *yellow dinosaur steamshovels were grunting*
> *as they cropped up tons of mush and grass*
> *to gouge their underworld garage.*
>
> *Parking spaces luxuriate like civic*
> *sandpiles in the heart of Boston.*
> *A girdle of orange, Puritan-pumpkin colored girders*
> *braces the tingling Statehouse.* (FUD)

"Boston State-House is the hub of the solar system," wrote Oliver Wendell Holmes. Lowell's Boston Statehouse is tingling with sterile vibrations, the opposite of electrical life. "Oh mama, mama, like a trolley-pole / sparking at contact, her electric shock— / the power house!" exclaimed the mad Negro soldier, referring to his Fraulein; "Lieutenants squawked like chickens in her skirts" (LS). Colonel Shaw, though hierarchical as the lieutenants or as Uncle Devereux, "rejoices in man's lovely, / peculiar power to choose life and die"; like the author, he secretly sighs "for the dark downward and vegetating kingdom / of the fish and reptile" (FUD). There he can wearily relax from his unbending duty, his bond to the Puritan state: "He is out of bounds now." Boundless, oceanic, he keeps no rank nor station in the grave.

> Shaw's father wanted no monument
> except the ditch,
> where his son's body was thrown
> and lost with his 'niggers,'

in the final dissolution of all hierarchy. (FUD)

The wish for death, the uniformed authority, and the paradox of glamor that invests them are the subject of a later poem, "The Opposite House."[20] It appeared, like "Waking Early Sunday Morning," in the year that followed the publication of *For the Union Dead*; and it echoes the Civil War both in its title and in its connection with the Spanish Civil War. "*Viva la muerte!*" bitterly cries its ironic conclusion, voicing again the crucial paradox: "Long live death!" The voice, ostensibly, and like Colonel Shaw, "rejoices in man's lovely, / peculiar power to choose life and die." Here, however, the "lovely, / peculiar power" is connected with an armed police car, which, "plodding slower than a turtle," is like the "giant finned cars," whose terrible image concluded "For the Union Dead." "Deterrent terror!"

> All day the opposite house,
> an abandoned police stable,
> just an opposite house,
> is square enough . . . .
> . . . .

---

20. Robert Lowell, "The Opposite House," *New York Review of Books*, IV (April 8, 1965), 4. It became part of the sequence, "Near the Ocean," in the volume, *Near the Ocean* (1967), pp. 37-38.

pigeons ganging through
broken windows and cooing
like gangs of children tooting
empty bottles.

Tonight, though, I see it shine
in the Azores of my open window.
Its manly, old-fashioned lines
are gorgeously rectilinear.
It's like some firework to be fired
at the end of the garden party.
Some Spanish casa, luminous
with heraldry and murder,
marooned in New York.

A stringy policeman is crooked
in the doorway, one hand on his revolver.
He counts his bullets like beads.
Two on horseback sidle
the crowd to the curb.
A red light
whirls on the roof of an armed car,
plodding slower than a turtle.
Deterrent terror!
Viva la muerte! (NO)

"Long live death!" compresses the persistent paradox into a
phrase. But this particular phrase, this version of the paradox,
was the slogan of the Falangist General Millán Astray. Millán
Astray was a cripple who, as conqueror, represented armed
authority. Miguel de Unamuno denounced him, calling the
slogan "a necrophilous and senseless cry." (It proved to be
Unamuno's last lecture.)

. . . "Just now . . . I heard a necrophilous and senseless cry:
'Long live death.' And I, who have spent my life shaping paradoxes
which have aroused the uncomprehending anger of others, I must
tell you, as an expert authority, that this outlandish paradox is
repellent to me. General Millán Astray is a cripple. Let it be said
without any slighting undertone. He is a war invalid. So was
Cervantes. Unfortunately there are too many cripples in Spain just
now. And soon there will be more if God does not come to our aid.
It pains me to think that General Millán Astray should dictate the
pattern of mass psychology. A cripple who lacks the spiritual
greatness of a Cervantes is wont to seek ominous relief in causing

mutilation around him." At this, Millán Astray was unable to restrain himself any longer.

"*Abajo la Inteligencia!*" he shouted. "*Viva la muerte!*"[21]

Aside from its intrinsic interest, this digression into Unamuno's revolt may be justified by the comparison with Lowell's own. Mr. Lowell, as we have seen, was imprisoned as a felon, in the Second World War, for the unorthodox nature of his pacifism: like the Picasso of "Guernica," he objected in particular to the calculated bombing of civilians; and he did not elect the authorized (or conventionally "theological") grounds to explain his objection.

Again, writing for the *Partisan Review* symposium on the Cold War, in 1962, Lowell denounced not only all nations that possess (nuclear) bombs, but even the very establishment of the sovereign nations themselves: "No nation should possess, use, or retaliate with its bombs. I believe we should rather die than drop our own bombs. . . . The sovereign nations . . . are really obsolete."[22] And even this was not his last word. Mr. Lowell still had the *palabra* in April, 1965, once again denouncing the necrophiles in the irony concluding "The Opposite House."

But the poetic force of Lowell's denunciation of the terrible, here as always, depends on its intimate contact with the tender. The pair of lines in the second stanza, for example, "It's like some firework to be fired / at the end of the garden party," derives from this account of the imprisoned Falangist leader, José Antonio Primo de Rivera, which Hugh Thomas gives just two pages before the above passage about Millán Astray:

The repercussions of one event in particular extended over both sides of these battle lines. This was the trial of José Antonio in Alicante. The decision to bring the leader of the Falange to trial seems to have been inspired by the fear that, if the Republic collapsed, one of their chief enemies would go unscathed. As always, fear showed itself the father of ruthlessness. During the

21. Hugh Thomas, *The Spanish Civil War* (New York: Harper & Brothers, 1961), p. 354.
22. Lowell, in "The Cold War and the West," *Partisan Review*, XXIX (Winter, 1962), p. 47.

trial, a militiaman appeared as a witness for the prosecution. "Do you hate the defendant?" asked José Antonio, who was defending himself. "With all my heart," replied the witness. Dignified and eloquent throughout, the founder of the Falange was condemned to death. His brother Miguel and his brother's wife received a similar sentence. But José Antonio, with the chivalry which even his enemies have never denied him, appealed on their behalf. "Life is not a firework one lets off at the end of a garden party," he concluded.[23]

A similar tenderness and a similar terror animate "For the Union Dead," but with larger, more elaborate ambivalence. In the lines, "Its Colonel is as lean / as a compass-needle," that needle's north and south are not only the American Civil War factions (North and South) but the Spanish, the biblical, the world's poles. They are life and death as in "Lady Ralegh's Lament": ". . . Voyage? / Down and down; the compass needle dead on terror" (FUD).

For the creative embrace counterbalancing the destructive impulse—and letting "the Union Dead" mean *Liebestod*—consider "Night Sweat," the arresting poem that immediately precedes "For the Union Dead." It takes for its theme the sweat of poetic creation, or of renewal. In contrast with the rhymeless and meterless quatrains, its stanzas or sections move in the guise of two sonnets. (The "Night Sweat" of the *Notebook* is only the first of these.) Yet (in the second section) it manages to couple the received kind of poetry—the fine passage in which the "gray / skulled horses whinny for the soot of night"—with the homely shock of "cycle on your back," a phrase that puns the grotesque calisthenics of copulation:

> Work-table, litter, books and standing lamp,
> plain things, my stalled equipment, the old broom—
> . . . .
> for ten nights now I've felt the creeping damp
> float over my pajamas' wilted white . . .
> Sweet salt embalms me and my head is wet,
> everything streams and tells me this is right;
> my life's fever is soaking in night sweat—

23. Thomas, *Spanish Civil War*, p. 352.

> one life, one writing! But the downward glide
> and bias of existing wrings us dry—
> always inside me is the child who died,
> always inside me is his will to die—
> one universe, one body . . . in this urn
> the animal night sweats of the spirit burn.
>
> Behind me! You! Again I feel the light
> lighten my leaded eyelids, while the gray
> skulled horses whinny for the soot of night.
> I dabble in the dapple of the day,
> a heap of wet clothes, seamy, shivering,
> I see my flesh and bedding washed with light,
> my child exploding into dynamite,
> my wife . . . your lightness alters everything,
> and tears the black web from the spider's sack,
> as your heart hops and flutters like a hare.
> Poor turtle, tortoise, if I cannot clear
> the surface of these troubled waters here,
> absolve me, help me, Dear Heart, as you bear
> this world's dead weight and cycle on your back.
>
> (FUD)

Cycle is, of course, first of all a noun, recalling the Indian cyclical world with its image of the globe riding on the back of the tortoise. But when cycle is read as a verb, the turtle flips. The world turns into the poet, and the riding into copulation, or parturition; something like the "ball" of Marvell's poem begins to emerge:

> Let us roll all our strength and all
> Our sweetness up into one ball,
> And tear our pleasure with rough strife
> Through the iron gates of life:
> Thus, though we cannot make our sun
> Stand still, yet we will make him run.

And something like the quickly expiring bounces of a ball, or the monosyllabic staccato of Marvell's last line, may be felt at the end of "Night Sweat," where the last six syllables, after the strain of "this world's dead weight," whisper and expire something like a shudder in the loins.

"Night Sweat," for all its traditional form, may be seen, if I am right, to participate in a revising of the bounds of poetry—a breaking of Victorian taboos as well as of modern strictures against the banal in the early sixties. For a man who has undergone a number of "breakdowns," as Lowell has called them, this is doubtless more therapeutic than iconoclastic. ". . . Amid the complex, dull horrors of the 1960s," Lowell has said, "poetry is a loophole. It's a second chance of some sort: things that the age turns thumbs down on you can get out in poetry."[24] If I am right about the concluding image of "Night Sweat," for example, we may say of Robert Lowell as he said of Colonel Shaw: "He is out of bounds now." Boston, for both, was rigor mortis. The decorum of the proper Bostonian was the death of poetry, and the death as well of the other forms of life. The Puritan mentality of the "cold-eyed seedy fathers" (LWC) would purify the earth of life itself—to live the lie that White-head called the "fallacy of misplaced concreteness." As Lowell put it in "Between the Porch and the Altar":

> They lied,
> My cold-eyed seedy fathers when they died,
> Or rather threw their lives away, to fix
> Sterile, forbidding nameplates on the bricks
> Above a kettle. Jesus rest their souls!

(LWC)

Shortly after the publication of *Life Studies*, after five years of residence in a Back Bay Boston town house, Lowell and his second wife, Elizabeth Hardwick, left Boston to live in New York City.

Lowell's emancipation may be felt (for another example) in " 'To Speak of Woe That Is in Marriage,' " which precedes "Skunk Hour" in *Life Studies*. The title quotes the Wife of Bath; the epigraph quotes Schopenhauer. Schopenhauer and the Wife of Bath! It is typical of Lowell to juxtapose such opposites—the pessimist of pessimists with that optimist of optimists, this male figure from the world of fact with that female figure from the world of fiction—and the latter twice as solid as the former. These associations are among the elements

24. Lowell, quoted in the *Time* Cover Story on Robert Lowell, *Time*, LXXIX, 22 (June 2, 1967), 67. The reference to the "breakdowns" is on p. 73.

that come together in the poem's ambivalent figure of copulation:

> "The hot night makes us keep our bedroom windows
> open.
> Our magnolia blossoms. Life begins to happen.
> My hopped up husband drops his home disputes,
> and hits the streets to cruise for prostitutes
>
> . . . .
> Oh the monotonous meanness of his lust. . . .
> It's the injustice . . . he is so unjust—
> whiskey-blind, swaggering home at five.
> My only thought is how to keep alive.
> What makes him tick? Each night now I tie
> ten dollars and his car key to my thigh. . . .
> Gored by the climacteric of his want,
> he stalls above me like an elephant." (LS)

The pitiless simultaneity of the mechanical, bestial and human, which are compacted by the raw ambivalence of *stalls*, grounds the elephant and the turtle (and the giant, finned cars) in a matrix of rediscovered candor—an America, a new found land. " 'To Speak of Woe,' " furthermore, is fourteen lines long, as are each of the two sections of "Night Sweat"; and the opening lines as well as the climactic image of the latter poem reverberate those of the former. (Algonquian myth makes Turtle the bearer of the earth; and Hindu myth makes the turtle and a serpent rest upon an elephant, while they bear, together, the earth.)[25]

Hence the epigraph of " 'To Speak of Woe' " may serve both

25. According to Alfred Métraux, the turtle is "a fairly prominent being in North American Indian mythology and religious beliefs, especially for tribes living east of the Mississippi River. The Iroquois hold the belief that the earth rests on the back of Turtle . . . the Delaware, also, say that the turtle is 'he who carries our mother's (the earth's) body.' . . . Other Algonquian-speaking tribes also make Turtle the bearer of the earth. . . ." ("Turtle," *Funk & Wagnall's Standard Dictionary of Folklore, Mythology, and Religion* [New York: Funk & Wagnalls Co., 1950], II, 1133.) In Asia, too, "the turtle is one of the mythical animals on which the earth rests," according to the *Encyclopaedia of Religion and Ethics*, (ed. J. Hastings [New York: Charles Scribner's Sons, 1908]), in the article, "Animals," by N. W. Thomas (I, 491 and 530): "In India we find various myths; one account gives the snake, another the elephant, as the world-bearing beast. . . . Another Hindu myth makes both turtle and serpent (dragon) rest upon an elephant . . ." while bearing, together, the earth.

poems and foreshadow the image of birth underlying "Night Sweat." " 'It is the future generation that presses into being by means of these exuberant feelings and super-sensible soap bubbles of ours.' Schophenhauer."[26]

Now, Schopenhauer, in the Fourth Book of *The World as Will and Idea*—"The Assertion and Denial of the Will to Live"—provides a gloss not only for "Night Sweat" but also, by extension, for "For the Union Dead" and the rest of Lowell's work:

> ... Birth and death belong in like manner to life, and hold the balance as reciprocal conditions of each other, or, if one likes the expression, as poles of the whole phenomenon of life. The wisest of all mythologies, the Indian, expresses this by giving to the very god that symbolises destruction, death (as Brahma, the most sinful and the lowest god of the Trimurti, symbolises generation, coming into being, and Vishnu maintaining or preserving), by giving, I say, to Siva as an attribute not only the necklace of skulls, but also the lingam, the symbol of generation, which appears here as the counterpart of death, thus signifying that generation and death are essentially correlatives, which reciprocally neutralize and annul each other.[27]

That squirrel wheel of birth, copulation, and death is one meaning of "this world's dead weight and cycle . . . ," but there is more. Not only the necklace of skulls but also the symbol of generation appear in the poem respectively as "the gray / skulled horses that whinny for the soot of night," and "my child exploding into dynamite." The tortoise, moreover, is a conventional representation of Vishnu, and of the *massa confusa* of the alchemical opus, according to Jung. "Night Sweat" is like a mandala. Enclosed in an emblematic triangle this mandala, this conjunction of opposites or *mysterium coniunc-*

26. Schopenhauer, according to Louis MacNeice's *Astrology* (New York: Doubleday & Company, 1964), p. 103, shares with Hölderlin and Nijinsky, who both went mad, the sun-sign Pisces. Lowell, who wrote the line, "My mind's not right," was also born under Pisces and refers to it—"*my month Pisces*"—in "To Allen Tate I," *Notebook 1967–68* (New York: Farrar, Straus & Giroux, 1969). Lowell probably knows MacNeice's book. He dedicates a poem to him in the *Notebook*: "The House-Party (For Louis MacNeice, 1907–1963)."

27. Arthur Schopenhauer, *The World as Will and Idea*, trans. R. B. Haldane and J. Kemp (Garden City, N.Y.: Doubleday & Company [Dolphin Books], 1961 [1818]), pp. 287–88.

tionis, is shown in a "Trimurti-picture" discussed by Jung: "The triangle symbolizes the tendency of the universe to converge towards the point of unity. The tortoise represents Vishnu; the lotus growing out of the skull between two flames, Shiva. The shining sun of Brahma forms the background. The whole picture corresponds to the alchmeical *opus,* the tortoise symbolizing the *massa confusa,* the skull the *vas* of transformation, and the flower the 'self' or wholeness."[28] Tortoise, skull, and shining sun appear clearly in Mr. Lowell's poem; but where is the flower, the " 'self' or wholeness"? There is no literal flower; but there is an image of birth, present by ambivalence, at the end of "Night Sweat," with *bear* meaning "produce" as well as "carry." ("Beyond the Alps," in *Life Studies,* makes a similar pun on birth: "the blear-eyed ego kicking in my berth / lay still, and saw Apollo plant his heels / on terra firma through the morning's thigh. . . .") When *cycle* flips from noun to verb, the human tortoise assumes the posture of copulation *and parturition;* the "child exploding into dynamite" disintegrates and is reborn, all at once. The flower, the new " 'self' or wholeness," is implicit in this rebirth.

It is clear that all this freight was not consciously planned; much of its detail is simply possible suggestiveness. The things in the poem are first of all just what they are, and not some other thing. Regarding an earlier version of the analysis, Mr. Lowell wrote: "The child exploding into dynamite was just the rather frightening early morning energy of a little girl and the blinding early sunlight. I rather wish I had meant the end you suggest, but fear I didn't—I had the old turtle who holds up the earth in mind."[29] But in the same paragraph he also acknowledged: ". . . my ear turns up things reason is unaware of." And some years ago in the "Skunk Hour" symposium, he wrote: "What I didn't intend often seems now at least as valid as what I did."[30]

28. C. G. Jung, *Psychology and Alchemy,* trans. R. F. C. Hull (New York: Pantheon Books [Bollingen], 1959), p. 148.

29. Robert Lowell, in a letter to me dated July 13, 1967.

30. Lowell, in the symposium "On Robert Lowell's 'Skunk Hour,' " in Anthony Ostroff (ed.), *The Contemporary Poet as Artist and Critic: Eight Symposia* (Boston: Little, Brown & Company, 1964), p. 107.

"Night Sweat" is an extremely private, extremely personal disclosure, about a dark night and emergence into morning. Its peculiar authenticity gives it the universal resonance of myth. It is not only the individual but the world that is remade, reborn in the action of the poem—"the old turtle who holds up the earth." As Lowell puts it: "One universe, one body." (We have already seen the central position of the shorter "Night Sweat" in the mythic year of the *Notebook*.) The myth of "Night Sweat" is cosmogonic. "Now we know," writes Jung in *Aion*, "that the cosmogonic myths are, at bottom, symbols for the coming of consciousness. . . . The dawn-state corresponds to the unconsciousness; in alchemical terms, it is the chaos, the *massa confusa* or *nigredo*; and by means of the opus, which the adept likens to the creation of the world, the *albedo* or *dealbatio* is produced, the whitening, which is compared sometimes to the full moon, sometimes to sunrise. It also means illumination, the broadening of consciousness that goes hand in hand with the 'work.' "[31] But of course the illumination is relative, transitory, ambivalent: "Poor turtle, tortoise, if I cannot clear / the surface of these troubled waters here, / absolve me. . . ."

Lowell's turtle—"Poor turtle, tortoise"—is first of all simply a term of endearment. It is comparable, in its climactic position in the poem, in the tenderness it condenses out of the poem's wider travail, and in its immediate matrix of confusion—it is comparable to the "Ah, love . . . !" of Arnold's "Dover Beach." But the resemblance only calls attention to the difference between the two poems. For Lowell's "Poor turtle" touches the casual, the nucleus of the colloquial—and at the moment of the poem's widest, most mythical reach. Both poems reach their climax in a very personal, lyric outcry; but Lowell's is more homely, pitched lower, and with correspondingly greater integrity. Not even the mansion of Crazy Jane is pitched any lower. Here in a plain tent of bed sheets, in naked disclosure, Lowell gets down to the plain truth, both in the colloquial diction and the bodily matter. He gets down to

31. C. G. Jung, *Aion: Researches into the Phenomenology of the Self*, trans. R. F. C. Hull (New York: Pantheon Books [Bollingen], 1959), p. 148.

turtle-flesh, the well-bottom, the here and now; he gets down at last to that Yeatsian place where all the ladders start.

And simultaneously the turtle supports the widest of mythic extension. The mythology of the tortoise is summarized by Kerenyi as follows:

> ... It is one of the oldest animals known to mythology. The Chinese see in it the mother, the veritable mother of all animals. The Hindus hold Kasyapa in honor, the "tortoise-man," father of their eldest gods, and say that the world rests on the back of a tortoise, a manifestation of Vishnu: dwelling in the nethermost regions, it supports the whole body of the world. The Italian name *tartaruga* keeps alive a designation dating from late antiquity, according to which the tortoise holds up the lowest layer of the universe, namely Tartarus ($\tau\alpha\rho\tau\alpha\rho\text{o}\nu\chi\text{os}$). Further . . . the tortoise like the dolphin is one of the shapes of Apollo. . . . Hermes makes it into a lyre. . . . For the Greeks the birth of the divine child, in his capacity as Eros Proteurhythmos, signified the rhythmic-musical quality of the world . . . the connection of water, child, and music.[32]

The connection of water, child, and the lyre of the poet's work relates "Night Sweat" to the archetypes of Jung and Kerenyi; this needs no further laboring. But the central paradox, the heart of the matter, which is carried in Lowell's figure of the turtle, needs all the elucidation it can get. The quotations from Schopenhauer, Jung, and Kerenyi have each probed "Night Sweat," including the turtle; but the mystery is only deepened.

Lowell, furthermore, concludes two other poems with the same mysterious figure. In one the turtle is helpless, passive, pitiable; in the other, full of malice and righteous menace. They are, in the order just described, "The Neo-Classical Urn" and "The Opposite House." Both are as full of destruction as "Night Sweat" is of generation. Schopenhauer explained: "Generation and death are essentially correlatives, which reciprocally neutralise and annul each other." The mothering turtle of "Night Sweat" is, in "The Neo-Classical Urn," both the brain and the multiple victim of her child, the boy:

32. C. G. Jung and C. Kerenyi, *Essays on a Science of Mythology: The Myths of the Divine Child and the Divine Maiden*, trans. R. F. C. Hull (New York: Harper & Row, Publishers [Torchbooks], 1963 [1949]), pp. 57–58.

I rub my head and find a turtle shell
stuck on a pole,
each hair electrical
with charges, and the juice alive
with ferment. Bubbles drive
the motor, always purposeful . . .
Poor head!
How its skinny shell once hummed

. . . .
. . . .   Rest!
I could not rest. At full run on the curve,
I left the caste stone statue of a nymph,
her soaring armpits and her one bare breast,
gray from the rain and graying in the shade,
as on, on, in sun, the pathway now a dyke,
I swerved between two water bogs,
two seins of moss, and stooped to snatch
the painted turtles on dead logs.
In that season of joy,
my turtle catch
was thirty-three,
dropped splashing in our garden urn,
like money in the bank,
the plop and splash
of turtle on turtle,
fed raw gobs of hash . . .

Oh neo-classical white urn, Oh nymph,
Oh lute! The boy was pitiless who strummed
their elegy,
for as the month wore on,
the turtles rose,
and popped up dead on the stale scummed
surface—limp wrinkled heads and legs withdrawn
in pain. What pain? A turtle's nothing. No
grace, no cerebration, less free will
than the mosquito I must kill—
nothings! Turtles! I rub my skull,
that turtle shell,
and breathe their dying smell,
still watch their crippled last survivors pass,
and hobble humpbacked through the grizzled grass. (FUD)

Those "crippled last survivors pass" like victims of some Hiroshima, or like "the spiders marching through the air, / Swim-
ming from tree to tree that mildewed day / In latter Au-

gust . . ." or the one Lowell watched, as a small boy, "whistle on a brick" (LWC).

We have already seen the turtle image concluding "The Opposite House": "an armed car, / plodding slower than a turtle. / Deterrent terror! / Viva la muerte!" The giant finned cars that conclude the Colonel Shaw poem are just as morbid. Thus, when Colonel Shaw leads his black soldiers to death, he is (in the words of "Beyond the Alps") "pure mind and murder at the scything prow." He seems to desire nothing so much as annihilation—for himself and for everyone else as well. He embodies the "old Abolitionist spirit," as Lowell made clear in his letter; but when he "seems to wince at pleasure, / and suffocate for privacy," it is the privacy of the grave he would have. Colonel Shaw is a Puritan victim of himself; "he waits / for the blessed break." And when he leads his black soldiers to death, his unbending resolution is again ambivalent. It enforces the morbid hierarchy it would abolish.

The very constitution of the United States is under question.[33] A contemporary Negro leader has put it this way: "We cannot be expected any longer to march and have our heads broken in order to say to whites: come on, you're nice guys. For you are not nice guys. We have found you out."[34] To this charge, "For the Union Dead" would enter a plea of guilty: but guilty of institutionalizing guilt. For the Calvinist idea of guilt, the Puritan abstraction, has hardened into the forms of the American abstraction, and perpetuates the radical starvation it has sought to eradicate.

Colonel Shaw, "as lean / as a compass needle," and the "stone statues of the abstract Union soldier," are figures of that abstraction, that starvation. Compare Allen Tate's analysis of the

33. Professor Loren Baritz explains how, in the form of abstraction, tyranny survived the American Revolution. The Puritans "did not kill the idea of the King's second body; they did not deny loyalty to the abstraction of the state. They had moved the abstraction to the new world with themselves and their Charter." (Loren Baritz, City on a Hill: A History of Ideas and Myths in America [New York: John Wiley & Sons, 1964], p. 44.)

34. Stokeley Carmichael, "What We Want," New York Review of Books, VII (September 22, 1966), 5.

abstract New England mind and William Alfred's metaphor of evil as a form of starvation. Here is Allen Tate:

> . . . For New England was one of those abstract-minded, sharp-witted trading societies that must be parasites in two ways: They must live economically on some agrarian class or country, and they must live spiritually likewise. New England lived economically on the South, culturally on England. And this created doubtless a disguised and involved nostalgia for the land—the New England "land" being old England. The homes and the universities of New England became a European museum, stuffed with the dead symbols of what the New Englander could not create because provision for it had been left out of his original foundation.[35]

And here is William Alfred's Kathleen, in *Hogan's Goat:*

> That's what evil is,
> The starvation of a heart with nothing in it
> To make the world around it nothing too.[36]

The dedication of *For the Union Dead* is "For my friend, William Alfred."

Hence the dark, lawless but vital forces which have been suppressed and therefore not comprehended smolder beneath the sweet volcanic cone. Hence Colonel Shaw, riding the world bubble, "waits / for the blessed break" (FUD). He wants the deluge. He is Lowell's monster, or Lowell himself.

The bubble is fame, illusion, the veil of Maya, the world, the life of appearances. As an annihilation of the veil of Maya, "the blessed break" of Colonel Shaw's bubble corresponds, for example, to the tearing of "the black web from the spider's sack" in "Night Sweat." The break was, is, will be, relief, release: "He is out of bounds now." He is liberated from the rigidities of his military self, his life, and from the binding, constipating, constricting sphincter of Boston, "the spun world's Hub" (as Lowell bitterly called it in "The Boston Nativity," in *Land of*

35. Allen Tate, "Remarks on the Southern Religion," in *I'll Take My Stand: The South and the Agrarian Tradition,* by Twelve Southerners (New York: Harper & Brothers, 1930), pp. 170–71.

36. William Alfred, *Hogan's Goat* (New York: Farrar, Straus & Giroux, 1966), p. 137.

Unlikeness) where the rainbow ends and where "serpents whistle at the cold"—Boston, the rigor mortis of the western world.

> *The stone statues of the abstract Union Soldier*
> *grow slimmer and younger each year—*
> *wasp-waisted, they doze over muskets*
> *and muse through their sideburns.* (*FUD*)

"The abstract Union Soldier"—*us*—grows more attenuated but becomes menacingly WASP-like, behind his white, Anglo-Saxon, Protestant, shut eyes, in an emblem of monumental indifference. The "break" is accordingly "blessed," and death takes the form of birth,[37] as it did for the heroic but dishonored Shaw when his body was "thrown and lost with his 'niggers' " (FUD). A bursting of the amnion, and an apocalyptic deluge in which giant finned cars slide by like monsters of the deep (a travesty of life, of every form of life, even of that elemental life of monstrous, mindless rapacity) is prepared by the fetal position in the lines before ("When I crouch to my television set, / the drained faces of Negro school-children rise like balloons"):

> *Shaw's father wanted no monument*
> *except the ditch*
> *where his son's body was thrown*
> *and lost with his 'niggers.'*
>
> *The ditch is nearer.*
> *There are no statues for the last war here;*
> *on Boylston Street, a commercial photograph*
> *shows Hiroshima boiling*
>
> *over a Mosler Safe, the "Rock of Ages"*
> *that survived the blast. Space is nearer.*
> *When I crouch to my television set,*
> *the drained faces of Negro school-children rise like balloons.*

37. Lowell associates birth and death with the Union through Lincoln: "Last spring I was talking about the Gettysburg Address to a friend who is also a man of letters. He pointed out to me its curious insistent use of birth images: 'brought forth,' 'conceived,' 'created,' and finally, a 'new birth of freedom.' Birth and Death!" (Robert Lowell, "On the Gettysburg Address," in Allan Nevins [ed.], *Lincoln and the Gettysburg Address: Commemorative Papers*, [Urbana: University of Illinois Press, 1964], pp. 88–89.)

Colonel Shaw
is riding on his bubble,
he waits
for the blessed break.

The Aquarium is gone. Everywhere,
giant finned cars nose forward like fish;
a savage servility
slides by on grease. (*FUD*)

Richard Poirier writes, "In Lowell's poetry such images are never only about Other People."[38]

The ambivalent "break" is also, of course, a figure of social change; and the metaphor is, in one of its moments, like this one by Robert L. Heilbroner: ". . . I also think that there are boundaries of change beyond which one cannot evolve but must burst, and I think it would take such a burst—such a political explosion—to propel us into the social economy Mr. Goodman writes about."[39] (Heilbroner is reviewing Paul Goodman's *People or Personnel.*) But at the same time that it suggests "political explosion," the breaking bubble is the mythical earth itself—as we have seen—like the ball furiously smashed by the Negro in *The Old Glory.* The latter reading, again, is enforced by the neighboring lines—integrating the mythic and the mundane: "On Boylston Street, a commercial photograph / shows Hiroshima boiling / over a Mosler Safe, the 'Rock of Ages' / that survived the blast." The Mosler Safe, the "Rock of Ages" (the anal bank, the oral hymn) epitomizes the "New England commercial theocracy," in Jarrell's phrase, which Lowell personally knew and rebelled against.[40] The personal and the historical, the actual and the mythical, the poet's and the world's body are conjoined: "One life, one writing . . .

---

38. Richard Poirier, "Our Truest Historian" (review of *For the Union Dead*), *Book Week*, II (October 11, 1964), 1. (Eliot remarked that in Pound's *Cantos*, Hell is for Other People.)

39. Robert L. Heilbroner, "Utopia or Bust" (review of Paul Goodman's *People or Personnel*), *New York Review of Books*, IV (May 6, 1965), 13.

40. Randall Jarrell, *Poetry and the Age* (New York: Vintage Books, 1955), p. 190: "In 'Rebellion' the son seals 'an everlasting pact / With Dives to contract / The world that spread in pain'; but at last he rebels against his father and his father's New England commercial theocracy, and 'the world spread / When the clubbed flintlock broke my father's brain.'"

one universe, one body," proclaims "Night Sweat." Lowell, the thief, like Hermes, goes to and fro between the opposing worlds: the mythic and the mundane, the world of the high poetic and the here and now, the world of Jung and Kerenyi and that of Heilbroner.

"Going to and fro," like Yeats's "Vacillation," names the implicit motion as explicit theme. Lowell's title is from the Book of Job (I:7), where "the Lord said unto Satan, Whence comest thou?" and "Satan answered the Lord, and said, From going to and fro in the earth, and from walking up and down in it." (The words are repeated in the poem's closing stanza: "The love that moves the stars / moved you! It set you going to and fro / and up and down. . . .") The Book of Job as a whole is relevant for its existential, or anti-pious, features; a quest for authenticity moves the poem.

The quest is radical. The "pure gold, the root of evil, / sunshine that gave the day a scheme," on the nether shores of darkness, is the noble-ignoble, alchemical-homosexual, Platonic, Satanic autobiography and transmutation of the poet, in the vessel of the colloquial ear:

> It's authentic perhaps
> to have been there, if now
> you could loll on the ledge for a moment,
> sunning like a couple
> . . . .
>
> One step, two steps, three steps:
> the hot-dog and coca cola bar,
> the Versailles steps,
> the Puritan statue—
> if you could get through the Central Park
> by counting . . .
>
> But the intestines shiver,
> the ferry saloon thugs with your pain
> across the river—pain
> suffering without purgation,
> the back-track of the screw.
> But you had instants,

to give the devil his due—
he and you
once dug it all out of the dark
unconscious bowels of the nerves:
pure gold, the root of evil,
sunshine that gave the day a scheme.

And now? Ah Lucifer!
how often you wanted your fling
with those French girls, Mediterranean
luminaries, Mary, Myrtho, Isis—
as far out as the sphynx!
The love that moves the stars

moved you!
It set you going to and fro
and up and down—
If you could get loose
from the earth by counting
your steps to the noose . . . (FUD)

What is this poem doing? "Going to and fro"? But where, what for? "To and fro in the earth . . . and up and down in it"? "We were very tired, we were very merry— / We had gone back and forth all night on the ferry"?

But the intestines shiver,
the ferry saloon thugs with your pain
across the river—pain,
suffering without purgation,
the back-track of the screw.

The blunt puns (the ferry saloon thugs, the back-track of the screw) are congenial to Yeats's Crazy Jane (" 'But Love has pitched his mansion in / The place of excrement; / For nothing can be sole or whole / That has not been rent' "); but they are not in the mode of Edna St. Vincent Millay. To remember her "Recuerdo" is ironic, to put it mildly; her ferry is in total contrast with the one here.

Internal contrast is provided by the stanza before, with the decorous Versailles steps and the disciplinary Puritan statue— though of course the Puritan statue moves also (and primarily) against the Versailles steps, since they suggest a palace of pleasure, or "Paris, our black classic," in the phrase of "Beyond the

Alps." That stanza's enigmatic problem of getting through the
park ("if you could get through the Central Park / by counting
. . .") is elucidated by the puns of "the ferry saloon thugs" and
also by a comparably seductive park in Buenos Aires, in another
poem:

> . . . Along the sunlit cypress walks
> of the Republican martyrs' graveyard,
> hundreds of one-room Roman temples
> hugged their neo-classical catafalques.
>
> Literal commemorative busts
> preserved the frogged coats
> and fussy, furrowed foreheads
> of those soldier bureaucrats.
>
> By their brazen doors
> a hundred marble goddesses
> wept like willows. I found rest
> by cupping a soft palm to each hard breast.
>
> That night I walked the streets.
> My pinched feet bled in my shoes. In a park
> I fought off seduction from the dark
> python bodies of new world demigods. . . .
>
> (FUD)[41]

41. Robert Lowell, "Buenos Aires," *New York Review of Books*, I
(February, 1963), 3; reprinted in *The Review*, 8 (August, 1963), 34–35;
and, after considerable revision, included in *For the Union Dead* (New
York: Farrar, Straus & Giroux, 1964), pp. 60–61. Ehrenpreis, who noted
that *For the Union Dead* was published too late to be considered in his
chapter on "The Age of Lowell" in *American Poetry*, was very enthusiastic
about Lowell's first version of "Buenos Aires," calling it "one of his finest
new 'public' poems." "As usual," Ehrenpreis commented, "the images are
what make the poem work. This time they depend on the old partners,
love and war, Venus and Mars, united here by means of Peron's name
Juan [implied by 'Peron, / the nymphets' Don Giovanni'], which suggests
the Don Juan legend. Lowell, disgusted by the official facade of the city,
treats it as a depopulated, over-furnished opera set, which he contrasts with
the off-stage crowds of the real Argentina. The opera is of course *Don
Giovanni*; and the centre of the poem recapitulates history with dead
generals in white marble recalling Mozart's Commendatore. Instead of the
file of Don Juan's abandoned mistresses, we meet marble goddesses mourning deceased heroes; or sex and death joined in a skull-like obelisk. Instead
of the great lover in hell, we hear Peron bellowing from exile, the seducer
of his people.
"Among these scenes the poet moves on foot in a circular path, as
spectator or sufferer. He starts from and returns to his hotel, caressing

Like the ferry saloon thugs, these neo-satyrs, priapic and Argentine, are seductive homosexually, in contrast to the heterosexual pull of the thanatic goddesses. Another comparable predation is described in *Life Studies*, in "Words for Hart Crane":

> "*When the Pulitzers showered on some dope*
> *or screw who flushed our dry mouths out with soap,*
> *few people would consider why I took*
> *to stalking sailors, and scattered Uncle Sam's*
> *phoney gold-plated laurels to the birds.*
> *Because I knew my Whitman like a book,*
> *stranger in America, tell my country: I,*
> *Catullus redivivus, once the rage*
> *of the Village and Paris, used to play my role*
> *of homosexual, wolfing the stray lambs*
> *who hungered by the Place de la Concorde. . . .*"(LS)

Still another poem relevant to the Central Park of "Going to and fro" is one that bears the title "Central Park," which appeared in 1965:

> *. . . I watched the lovers occupy*
> *every inch of earth and sky:*
> *one figure of geometry,*
> *multiplied to infinity,*
> *straps down, and sunning openly . . .*
> *each precious, public, pubic tangle*
> *an equilateral triangle . . . .*

The poem concludes:

> *Oh Pharoahs starving in your foxholes,*
> *with painted banquets on the walls,*
> *fists knotted in your captives hair,*
> *tyrants with little food to spare—*
> *all your embalming left you mortal,*
> *glazed, black and hideously eternal,*
> *all your plunder and gold leaf*
> *only served to draw the thief . . .*

---

inanimate statutes (his muses) en route but speaking to nobody. Instead of virile love, he encounters homosexuals in a park; but like Donna Anna, though unlike Argentina, he fights off seduction. Fascinated as so often by what repels him, he sees the truth behind the scrim and delivers it to us by way of his conscience." (Ehrenpreis, "Age of Lowell," pp. 93–94.)

> We beg delinquents for our life.
> Behind each bush, perhaps a knife;
> each landscaped crag, each flowering shrub,
> hides a policeman with a club. (NO)[42]

The geometry here, the multiplicity of the erotic figures and "each precious, public, pubic tangle / an equilateral triangle," corresponds to the obsession with counting in "Going to and fro," and in the career of Don Juan, who is mentioned in a version of "Buenos Aires" ("Peron, / the nymphet's Don Giovanni"[43]). The fundamental contrast, of course, in "Central Park" as in "Buenos Aires" and "Going to and fro," moves between the poles of Eros and death: the lovers and the live pubes against the geometry and the mummies; the breasts and python bodies against the Republican martyrs' catafalques; the golden "instants" in "Going to and fro" against the Puritan statue and the sterile numbering of the steps.

Now this counting, this iterative motif in "Going to and fro," is very ambivalent, and it suggests a number of things. It suggests mutability, the numbers of time, the inexorable "simmer of rot and renewal" (FUD). But one thing it is bound to suggest, along with whatever else, is poetry itself: metrical lines, the art of composition in words—the art of "numbers." ("As yet a child, nor yet a fool to fame, / I lisped in numbers, for the numbers came," said Pope.) Therefore "Going to and fro," whatever else it does, enacts its own creation and is "about" poetry itself. The going to and fro, the counting of the steps, and the elusive "instants" all lend themselves perfectly well to the "story" of a poet, the parable of a man who writes verse. Numbers are linked with words by Lowell's Prometheus, as the twin elements of reason and the beginnings of human thought:

> I taught men the rising and the setting of the
> stars. From the stars, I taught them numbers.
> I taught women to count their children, and men
> to number their murders. I gave them the alphabet.

42. Robert Lowell, "Central Park," *New York Review of Books*, V (October 14, 1965), 3. It became part of the sequence, "Near the Ocean," in the volume *Near the Ocean* (1967), pp. 39–41.

43. Lowell, "Buenos Aires," *New York Review of Books*, p. 3.

> Before I made men talk and write with words, knowl-
> edge dropped like a dry stick into the fire of
> their memories, fed that fading blaze an instant,
> then died without leaving an ash behind. (PB)

But the conversion of experience into poetry, at least since the Romantics, has been regarded as a project whose success is characteristically intermittent: "But you had instants": the experience has tended to fade into the light of common day, and the elusiveness itself becomes a theme. So is it here. The golden instant is "out of this world," hence the wish to "get loose / from the earth." The conclusion of the poem, if I am right, grants the poet precious little success.

It is also, however, more complicated than that. "To mount for that beauty's sake ever upwards, as by a flight of steps, from one to two, and from two to all beautiful bodies . . . ," was the counsel of Diotima to Socrates, in Plato's notorious *Symposium*.[44] "One step, two steps, three steps": the beautiful bodies in the Central Park are being counted as Diotima counseled, as a *Gradus ad Parnassum* or mystical Way to the *Nous*:

> The love that moves the stars
>
> moved you!
> It set you going to and fro
> and up and down—
> If you could get loose
> from the earth by counting
> your steps to the noose . . .

Regarding the intentionality of this pun, Lowell wrote: "Some things are hard to tell—noose was just a noose as far as I know, but my ear turns up things reason is unaware of. I was thinking in that poem of Nerval, who had manic depressive hallucinations and did end up that way."[45] Nerval hanged himself at the

44. Plato, the *Symposium* (211c), in *Great Dialogues of Plato*, trans. W. H. D. Rouse (New York: New American Library [Mentor Books], 1956), p. 105.

45. Mr. Lowell, in a letter to me dated June 13, 1967. For another occurrence of the figure of the noose, consider the metaphor with which he concluded his address as winner of a National Book Award, on March 23, 1960: "When I finished *Life Studies*, I was left hanging on a question-mark. I am still hanging there. I don't know whether it is a death-rope or a life-line."

bottom of some stone stairs. Lowell pictures him walking down the steps to tighten the noose. Nerval's graduated descent makes a Satanic, mirror image of the mystical ladder to the Nous. But in any case, the steps to the noose correspond to the "ten / steps of the roaring ladder," in the opening stanza of "Waking Early Sunday Morning":

> O to break loose, like the chinook
> salmon jumping and falling back,
> nosing up to the impossible
> stone and bone-crushing waterfall—
> raw-jawed, weak-fleshed there, stopped by ten
> steps of the roaring ladder, and then
> to clear the top on the last try,
> alive enough to spawn and die. (NO)

In both cases, annihilation is ambivalently sexual and hence paradoxically fulfilling.

The *Nous* is, according to Hermes Trismegistus, hermaphroditic.[46] If there is a further pun on *noose*, it unites heaven and earth: from the merely smutty to the ultra cosmic. "L'amor che move il sole e l'altre stelle": "The love that moves the stars"— that concluded Dante's *Paradiso*—"moved you!" "It set you going to and fro and up and down"—in a perfectly carnal motion. The ubiquitous ambivalence of poetry underlies all movement—or vice-versa. Delmore Schwartz wrote of love's opposite, hate, moving the stars—as in the Empedoclean oscillation of the universe between love and hate, or as in the movement of negation in Hegel's dialectic:

> . . . in the end
> All men may seem essential boxers, hate
> May seem the energy which drives the stars,
> (L'amor che move il sole e l'altre stelle!)
> And war as human as the beating heart:
> So Hegel and Empedocles have taught.[47]

Jung notes that "the antithetical nature of the *ens primum* is an almost universal idea. In China the opposites are yang and yin,

46. C. G. Jung, *Psychology and Alchemy*, p. 318, n. 38: "Hermes Trismegistus: The Nous is Hermaphroditic."

47. Delmore Schwartz, *Shenandoah* (Norfolk, Conn.: New Directions Pub. Corp., 1941), p. 20. Shenandoah speaks.

odd and even numbers, heaven and earth, etc.: there is also a
union of them in the hermaphrodite."[48] But the Nous of
"Going to and fro" is a noose, deadly or throttling, like a
constricting sphincter: sphinx, in the phrase "as far out as the
Sphynx," is cognate with sphincter—though Lowell writes that
he did not intend the pun.[49] This Nous, like "Minerva the
mis-carriage of the brain" in "Beyond the Alps" (FUD) and
like Goethe's Mephistophelean "Geist, der stets verneint," is as
diabolical as the hangman's noose in "The Ferris Wheel," in
Lord Weary's Castle:

> This world, this ferris wheel, is tired and strains
> Its townsman's humorous and bulging eye,
> As he ascends and lurches from his seat
> And dangles by a shoe-string overhead
> To tell the racing world that it must die.
> Who can remember what his father said?
> The little wheel is turning on the great
> In the white water of Christ's blood. The red
> Eagle of Ares swings along the lands,
>
> Of camp-stools where the many watch the sky:
> The townsman hangs, the eagle swings. It stoops
> And lifts the ferris wheel into the tent
> Pitched for the devil. But the man works loose,
> He drags and zigzags through the circus hoops,
> And lion-taming Satan bows and loops
> His cracking tail into a hangman's noose;
> He is the only happy man in Lent.
> He laughs into my face until I cry. (LWC)

Noose suggests the constriction or strangulation enforced by the
Lenten, gloomy New England conscience; but it also implies, in
"The Ferris Wheel," the cycle of the wheel—the inexorable law
of mutability, with its cycles of birth and death ("To tell the
racing world that it must die"). Both Calvinist rigor and its
festive opposite seem to confine life in this poem: "Which way
I fly is Hell," says Milton's Satan; "myself am Hell." And so, in
"The Ferris Wheel," when "the man works loose," he becomes
confused with Satan: "he" is both "Satan" and "I."

48. Jung, Psychology and Alchemy, p. 318, n.38.
49. Robert Lowell, in a letter to me dated June 13, 1967.

> And lion-taming Satan bows and loops
> His cracking tail into a hangman's noose;
> He is the only happy man in Lent.
> He laughs into my face until I cry.

He is another version of Lowell's monster.

Ferris wheel, Satan's tail, and hangman's noose may even correspond to the ferry (fairy), sphinx (sphincter) and noose (Nous) of the later poem. The rebellion against the puritan constraint, whether the constraint be Catholic or Protestant, is constant; but the range of associations, particularly the invasion of the colloquial, has developed until the later poem is . . . "as far out as the sphynx!"

For "Going to and fro" moves as if inside the occult tradition —as if animated, albeit semiconsciously, by a satanism like that of Baudelaire's *Fleurs du Mal.* "*Les Fleurs du Mal* is a recounting of the great descent," according to John Senior, in his study, *The Way Down and Out: The Occult in Symbolist Literature.* "Baudelaire wallows in the slough of 'Satan Trismégiste,' the Logos; and like Heraclitus in reverse, he declares that the way down is the way up. Baudelaire's Satan, like Blake's and Hugo's, must be lived through; he cannot be denied or jumped over."[50]

> And now? Ah Lucifer!
> how often you wanted your fling
> with those French girls, Mediterranean
> luminaries, Mary, Myrtho, Isis—

cries the voice of "Going to and fro"—to himself; yet not about himself, but about Nerval and Lucifer. Lowell again conflates the personal and the mythic. The *pot pourri* of "fallen" "luminaries"—Christian- Greek- and Egyptian-named "French girls" —suggest the triple goddess herself. Their polyglot names measure perhaps the globe-trotting energy, or rut, of the satanic "Going to and fro."

Yet above all the poem is a simple lyric. The sentence beginning "But you had instants" is comparable, in poignancy, to the lyric outcry of "Waking Early Sunday Morning":

50. John Senior, *The Way Down and Out: The Occult in Symbolist Literature* (Ithaca, N.Y.: Cornell University Press, 1959), p. 92.

O to break loose. All life's grandeur
is something with a girl in summer. . . . (NO)

And, in its paradoxically more astringent, flatter, more under-stated way, "Going to and fro" is as poignant as Auden's lyric "Lay your sleeping head, my love"—and it has a comparable theme.

But you had instants,

to give the devil his due—
he and you
once dug it all out of the dark
unconscious bowels of the nerves:
pure gold, the root of evil,
sunshine that gave the day a scheme.

That is in the middle of Lowell's poem; compare it with the conclusion of Auden's:

Beauty, midnight, vision dies:
Let the winds of dawn that blow
Softly round your dreaming head
Such a day of sweetness show
Eye and knocking heart may bless,
Find the mortal world enough;
Noons of dryness see you fed
By the involuntary powers.
Nights of insult let you pass
Watched by every human love.[51]

"Going to and fro," then, for all its occult vibrations, is a lyric gesture of existential simplicity. The lines "If you could get loose / from the earth by counting / your steps to the noose. . ." imply a lyric recognition of the human predicament, I believe, such as Victor Hugo expressed and Pater quoted: "Well! we are all condamnés, as Victor Hugo says: we are all under sentence of death but with a sort of indefinite reprieve—*les hommes sont tous condamnés à mort avec des sursis indéfinis. . . .*" In an opposite mood—still lyric, but savage—Lowell renders Baude-laire's "Au lecteur" on the same death-sentence, the same "guil-lotine," in *Imitations*:

51. W. H. Auden, "Lay your sleeping head, my love," *The Collected Poetry of W. H. Auden* (New York: Random House, 1945), p. 209.

> . . . If poison, arson, sex, narcotics, knives
> have not yet ruined us and stitched their quick,
> loud patterns on the canvas of our lives,
> it is because our souls are still too sick.
>
> Among the vermin, jackals, panthers, lice,
> gorillas and tarantulas that suck
> and snatch and scratch and defecate and fuck
> in the disorderly circus of our vice,
>
> there's one more ugly and abortive birth.
> It makes no gestures, never beats its breast,
> yet it would murder for a moment's rest,
> and willingly annihilate the earth.
>
> It's BOREDOM. Tears have glued its eyes together.
> You know it well, my Reader. This obscene
> beast chain-smokes yawning for the guillotine—
> you—hypocrite Reader—my double—my brother! (IMIT)

You, hypocrite Reader, my double, my brother: you are Lowell's monster. It is I.

The beast chain-smoking, yawning for the guillotine or the noose,

> . . . cannot discover America by counting
> the chains of condemned freight-trains
> from thirty states,

in "The Mouth of the Hudson." Neither, in the poem that follows it, "Fall 1961," can he comprehend the ticking clock as progress:

> Back and forth, back and forth
> goes the tock, tock, tock
> of the orange, bland, ambassadorial
> face of the moon
> on the grandfather clock.
>
> All autumn, the chafe and jar
> of nuclear war;
> we have talked our extinction to death.
> I swim like a minnow
> behind my studio window.
>
> Our end drifts nearer,
> the moon lifts,
> radiant with terror.
> The state
> is a diver under a glass bell.

A father's no shield
for his child.

.   .   .   .

Nature holds up a mirror.
One swallow makes a summer.
It's easy to tick
off the minutes,
but the clockhands stick. (FUD)

"There will once more, as so often in the past, be change but no progress": failing comprehension of the monster, as Collingwood warns, we stick in a rut: "the clockhands stick." "And we ought by now to realize that no kindly law of nature will save us from the fruits of our ignorance."[52] "Fall 1961" concludes:

Back and forth!
Back and forth, back and forth—
my one point of rest
is the orange and black
oriole's swinging nest! (FUD)

The going to and fro is all there is. "Nature holds up a mirror," the nature of "Eye and Tooth": "a simmer of rot and renewal" (FUD). Here the stuffed toucan of "My Last Afternoon with Uncle Devereux Winslow" has become the American eagle—or hawk, whose "ascetic talon" is the bestial *lex talionis:*

. . . No ease from the eye
of the sharp-shinned hawk in the birdbook there,
with reddish brown buffalo hair
on its shanks, one ascetic talon

clasping the abstract imperial sky.
It says:
an eye for an eye,
a tooth for a tooth,

as in Vietnam; yet this is Lowell himself, personally, intimately:

No ease for the boy at the keyhole,
his telescope,
when the women's white bodies flashed
in the bathroom. Young, my eyes began to fail.

52. R. G. Collingwood, *The Idea of History* (London: Oxford University Press, 1946), p. 334.

> Nothing! no oil
> for the eye, nothing to pour
> on those waters or flames.
> I am tired. Everyone's tired of my turmoil. (FUD)

The poem evidently evolved from (or was cognate with) a prose meditation on William Carlos Williams which Lowell published a few years before For the Union Dead. The prose somewhat expands and further specifies the poem's arresting figure of the summer rain, falling in pinpricks, a simmer of rot and renewal (and elemental suggestiveness, like the snow falling all over Ireland, "upon all the living and the dead," at the end of Joyce's "The Dead"); the "triangular blotch / of rot on the red roof," and the "sharp-shinned hawk in the birdbook there, / with reddish brown buffalo hair / on its shanks, one ascetic talon / clasping the abstract imperial sky"; and, in the whiteness of the lovably vulnerable house, perhaps the whiteness of the women's bodies (spied through the bathroom keyhole once by a young but guilty eye [I], which by the lex talionis of the New England conscience was already failing, although the boy was young):

> When I think about writing on Dr. Williams, I feel a chaos of thoughts and images, images cracking open to admit a thought, thoughts dragging their roots for the soil of an image. When I woke up this morning, something unusual for this summer was going on!—pinpricks of rain were falling in a reliable, comforting simmer. Our town was blanketed in the rain of rot and the rain of renewal. New life was muscling in, everything growing moved on its one-way trip to the ground. I could feel this, yet believe our universal misfortune was bearable and even welcome. An image held my mind during these moments and kept returning—an old fashioned New England cottage freshly painted white. I saw a shaggy, triangular shade on the house, trees, a hedge, or their shadows, the blotch of decay. The house might have been the house I was now living in, but it wasn't; it came from the time when I was a child, still unable to read and living in the small town of Barnstable on Cape Cod. Inside the house was a birdbook with an old stiff and steely engraving of a sharp-shinned hawk. The hawk's legs had a reddish brown buffalo fuzz on them; behind was the blue sky, bare and abstracted from the world. In the present, pinpricks of rain were falling on everything I could see, and even on the white house in my mind, but the hawk's picture, being indoors

I suppose, was more or less spared. Since I saw the picture of the hawk, the pinpricks of rain have gone on, half the people I once knew are dead, half the people I now know were then unborn, and I have learned to read.[53]

One thinks of Williams' poem, "By the road to the contagious hospital," as an analogue and possibly as an imagistic source for Lowell's evocation here of the creative process—and of the universal "simmer of rot and renewal." The conjunction of creation and destruction is the ambivalent key. In "Eye and Tooth," however, the tone of despair would prevail—but for the triumphant playfulness of the punning. Irvin Ehrenpreis describes this very well, although where he says "humor," I would say "gallows-humor"; and it seems to me that he possibly overlooks the concluding pun. Ehrenpreis writes:

. . . "Eye and Tooth," a skillful extraction of humour from despair, illustrates a truism about middle age: viz. that so far from bringing us serenity, the years leave us naked; only we learn, not without some disgust, that the self can survive even the shabbiest humiliation. The poem depends on a brilliant use of the eye-I pun. Treating vision as memory or id, Lowell presents the voyeur poet's eye as an unwreckable showcase of displeasing memories that both shape and torment the person. The dominating metaphor is, so to speak, "I've got something in my I and I can't get it out." Towards the end Lowell neatly ties the public to the domestic by implying that just as his readers observe his gestures with unease provoked by their own recollections, so his familiars must in the routines of living find his condition hardly more bearable than he does:

Nothing! no oil
for the eye, nothing to pour
on those waters or flames.
I am tired. Everyone's tired of my turmoil.[54]

The analogy Ehrenpreis shows us in the conclusion is ingenious, whereas the final pun is almost too homely to mention. But it may be that this very homeliness, and maybe a priapic playfulness, inhabiting the poem's last word, *turmoil*—in which the artist's ivory tower and Lord Weary's feudal castle, in the German of the syllable *Turm*, are together brought low—accord

53. Robert Lowell, "William Carlos Williams," *Hudson Review*, XIV (Winter, 1961–62), 530–31.
54. Ehrenpreis, "Age of Lowell," p. 94.

it the position of triumph, as the last word. Its *oil* was made to be separated three lines before.

Lowell's puns are no ordinary matter; or rather, they tap the nucleus of the ordinary. The drab, "unforgivable landscape," in the raw, spontaneous allegory of "The Mouth of the Hudson," with the Negro reduced to a hobo, has the pride of his ancestral tom-tom, together with all the energy that was figured in the "trolley-pole / sparking at contact," in "A Mad Negro Soldier Confined at Munich"—has this much movement (and a short history of communications) comprehended by the homeliest of puns, "a discarded, gray/Westinghouse Electric cable drum." It moves, of course, only in the special field of the poem's excitement—and with typical understatement, subtlety, and compression. "The Mouth of the Hudson," quoted in Chapter I (pages 10–11), is a good example of Lowell's new, minimal, emergent form.

The mouth of the Hudson is the mouth of Hell and the poet's mouth: it is scorched by Avernal ("birdless") gases, but its desolation speaks, through the conscience of the poem, with the grace at least to condemn itself ambivalently. For the way up and the way down are one and the same, and the simmer of rot is concurrently a simmer of renewal, in the figure of the hobo Negro toasting wheat-seeds. *For the landscape is a monstrous figure of the desolate artist.* This poem's premise is like that of *Paterson*: "that a man in himself is a city . . . all the details of which may be made to voice his most intimate convictions." Here mouth of the lordly Hudson, descended to such ruin, utters the exilic poem *de profundis*. Its concluding figure, the ironical evocation of sunbathers, is a mingling of the opposite tones of whimsy and outrage, in what can be taken as a virtual or implied pun: sunbathing is a form of recreation, or re-creation, but the factories are unforgivably destructive.

The point barely emerges. The ice drifts seaward. Lowell's perspective finally is neither tragic nor comic, sacred nor profane, mythic nor mortal, living nor dead, but the lyric, ambivalent emergency of both. The reader must act as a sort of midwife; his own participation completes the poem. He must go further still: he must discover *himself* in the figure of the artist—in the body of the poem that he has helped to form. Lowell's experimentation with minimal art is a sign of the times. Its context, in the broader cultural scene, has been sharply observed by Susan Sontag, in her essay, "The Aesthetics of Silence":

Perhaps the quality of the attention one brings to bear on something will be better (less contaminated, less distracted), the less one is offered. Furnished with impoverished art, purged by silence, one might then be able to begin to transcend the frustrating selectivity of attention, with its inevitable distortions of experience. Ideally, one should be able to pay attention to everything.

The tendency is toward less and less. But never has "less" so ostentatiously advanced itself as "more."

In the light of the current myth, in which art aims to become a "total experience," soliciting total attention, the strategies of impoverishment and reduction indicate the most exalted ambition art could adopt. Underneath what looks like a strenuous modesty, if not actual debility, is to be discerned an energetic secular blasphemy: the wish to attain the unfettered, unselective, total consciousness of "God."[55]

But that way silence lies.

55. Susan Sontag, *Styles of Radical Will* (New York: Farrar, Straus & Giroux, 1969), pp. 13–14.

❧ VII. NEAR THE OCEAN

O Hammerheaded Shark,
the Rainbow Salmon of the World, your hand
a rose . . .

ROBERT LOWELL

It is only by the destruction of forms that forms, in art or in life, are remade. It is only by the profanation of the sacred that the sacred can be renewed and permitted to renew and sanctify the profane. Stated baldly this is almost a commonplace; but the lively intuition of something like it is the principle of Lowell's life work. In the title sequence of the volume *Near the Ocean*, which opens with "Waking Early Sunday Morning," the principle emerges as a theme: "O to break loose . . . spawn and die."

The ocean of Lowell's title is the Pacific, the Atlantic, the final solution, the Flood, the resolving of all differences, the antithesis of hierarchy. It relates to the global sop in Shakespeare's *Troilus*:

> Take but degree away, untune that string,
> And hark what discord follows. Each thing meets
> In mere oppugnancy. The bounded waters
> Should lift their bosoms higher than the shores
> And make a sop of all this solid globe. . . .
> (I, iii, 109–113)

Lowell's ocean relates to that figure of chaos; but also to the figure of plenitude, the "oceanic" feeling Freud describes (refer-

ring to a letter of Romain Rolland's) near the beginning of
Civilization and its Discontents:

> . . . Originally the ego includes everything, later it separates off
> an external world from itself. Our present ego-feeling is, therefore,
> only a shrunken residue of a much more inclusive—indeed, an
> all-embracing—feeling which corresponded to a more intimate
> bond between the ego and the world about it. If we may assume
> that there are many people in whose mental life this primary
> ego-feeling has persisted to a greater or less degree, it would exist in
> them side by side with the narrower and more sharply demarcated
> ego-feeling of maturity, like a kind of counterpart to it. In that
> case, the ideational contents appropriate to it would be precisely
> those of limitlessness and of a bond with the universe—the same
> ideas with which my friend elucidated the "oceanic" feeling.[1]

Out of that plenary coherence, order emerges by means of
negation, and to it we return by the negation of order.

> Now, you honor the mother.
> Omnipresent,
> she made you nonexistent,
> the ocean's anchor, our high tide. (NO)

Thus concludes "For Theodore Roethke," sixth poem of the
volume *Near the Ocean* (1967). The oceanic plenitude of
mother earth means the annihilation or dissolution of individual flesh and bone. In the cryptic phrase "the ocean's anchor"
Lowell perhaps envisions the dead poet as the earth itself,
which does anchor the ocean against the pull of the moon, and
which is, in the hyperbolized substance of Theodore Roethke,
the elevation of all human achievement. The figure enacts the
Heraclitean doctrine that the way up and the way down are one
and the same.

Near the Ocean consists of seven original poems and six
translations. Five of the original poems are grouped under the
collective title "Near the Ocean," which is also the title of the
fifth poem. We have just seen the figure of the ocean in the
sixth poem, "For Theodore Roethke." The seventh and last of
the original poems, "1958," suggests the ocean with its "Ham-

---

1. Sigmund Freud, *Civilization and Its Discontents*, trans. James
Strachey (New York: W. W. Norton & Company, 1962), p. 15.

merheaded shark, / the rainbow salmon of the world," then concludes by suggesting the *opposite* of the ocean bottom, "the ocean's anchor":

> . . . *And at the Mittersill, you topped*
> *the ski-run, that white eggshell, your sphere, not land*
> *or water—no circumference anywhere,*
> *the center everywhere, I everywhere,*
> *infinite, fearful . . . standing—you escaped.* (NO)

"That white eggshell, your sphere," the top of the world, like the geomorphic figure in "For Theodore Roethke," is a sort of cosmic center where all opposites coincide. The poet, the lover, the speaker, finds himself in the role of God the Creator: "no circumference anywhere, / the center everywhere, I everywhere," echoing the dictum of St. Bonaventura that the nature of God, or Being, is "an intelligible sphere whose center is everywhere and whose circumference is nowhere."[2] In the *Notebook* version of the poem, an allusion to Pascal emerges, and the God-like person at the ubiquitous world-center is the woman the poem is addressed to: ". . . We stand. . . . / We ski-walked the eggshell at the Mittersill, / Pascal's infinite, perfect sphere— / the border nowhere, your center everywhere. . . ." The ecstatic ("We stand"), manic, all-centering power is indeterminately the poet's and the woman's, in their momentary union, standing on top of the world (ex + *histanai*—"spaced out") on a ski-run shaped like the cosmic egg. In the earlier version, the phrase "not land / or water," referring to the snow- (frozen water) topped mountain, reminds one of the indeterminacy of the slush, "not ice, not snow," in "The Exile's Return," with its analogy to the secular creator, Tonio Kröger. The motif of escape that opens and closes "1958" in *Near the Ocean*, together with its figure of the rainbow salmon, completes the opening words of the opening poem of the volume, "Waking Early Sunday Morning," whose theme is also escape, creation, and renewal:

2. Saint Bonaventura, *The Mind's Road to God*, trans. George Boas (New York: Liberal Arts Press, 1953), p. 38.

O to break loose, like the chinook
salmon jumping and falling back,
nosing up to the impossible
stone and bone-crushing waterfall—
raw-jawed, weak-fleshed there, stopped by ten
steps of the roaring ladder, and then
to clear the top on the last try,
alive enough to spawn and die. (NO)

The "ten / steps of the roaring ladder" are like Eliot's "figure of the ten stairs," in "Burnt Norton." Eliot derived his
figure from the *Dark Night of the Soul*, by Saint John of the
Cross, where Heraclitus's paradox is repeated: "For, upon this
road, to go down is to go up, and to go up, to go down. . . ."[3]
"This road" is again the mystical Way to the *Nous*. Saint John
of the Cross teaches an ancient secret: ". . . For he that hum-
bles himself is exalted and he that exalts himself is humbled."
The crucial point is emphasized by Eliot: "The detail of the
pattern is movement." And Lowell brings the secret movement
home: "O to break loose . . . spawn and die."

Lowell's salmon falls are like the salmon falls of "Sailing to
Byzantium," and they present a similar dilemma; but they do
not, as Yeats's do, lead to admiration (whether earnest or
ironic) of the transcendental. Lowell opts for the flux of the
here and now, as we have seen: "Oh to break loose. All life's
grandeur / is something with a girl in summer. . . ." This couplet climaxes the poem in the twelfth stanza, originally (in the
New York Review) the tenth—as if, with the tenth step of the
roaring ladder, "to clear the top on the last try, / alive enough
to spawn and die."

But the spawning corresponds, ironically, to the poet's creative action; and that, as we know, is something of a thanatic
affair. Ambivalence, accordingly, animates, structurally and in
detail, this fourteen-stanza poem about renewal.

Even the choice of the fourteen stanzas—given the religious
context of the title—suggests perhaps the fourteen stations of

3. Saint John of the Cross, *Dark Night of the Soul*, trans. E. Allison
Peers (Garden City, N.Y.: Doubleday & Company [Image Books], 1959),
Book II, chap. xviii, p. 165.

the cross, and with them their idea of an imitation of Christ. Christ was a notable teacher of the paradoxical Way Down; and his resurrection, on Sunday morning, like the break of day, is traditionally interpreted as a paradigm of all renewal. The suggestion moves with irony, of course, in a poem whose burden is the fruitlessness of Christians and the sterility of the dead wooden cross. But the ambivalence is genuine and motile; the destructive irony tempers authentic renewal.

> *Time to grub up and junk the year's*
> *output, a dead wood of dry verse:*
> *dim confession, coy revelation,*
> *liftings, listless self-imitation,*
> *whole days when I could hardly speak,*
> *came pluming home unshaven, weak*
> *and willing to read anyone*
> *things done before and better done.*[4]

That is the way the third stanza first appeared, in the *New York Review of Books*; Lowell changed it to read as follows, in *Near the Ocean*:

> *Vermin run for their unstopped holes;*
> *in some dark nook a fieldmouse rolls*
> *a marble, hours on end, then stops;*
> *the termite in the woodwork sleeps—*
> *listen, the creatures of the night*
> *obsessive, casual, sure of foot,*
> *go on grinding, while the sun's*
> *daily remorseful blackout dawns.* (NO)

This new version is less explicit, more metaphoric; the poet's need for renewal is couched in the figures of the ignoble night-creatures.

The materials for the renewal are the forlorn hope of a junk heap, like Yeats's "Old kettles, old bottles, and a broken can, / Old iron, old bones, old rags . . ." in "The Circus Animals' Desertion." Lowell's eighth stanza, in particular, seems to echo Yeat's "shop": "No, put old clothes on, and explore / the

---

4. Robert Lowell, "Waking Early Sunday Morning," *New York Review of Books*, V (August 5, 1965), 3.

corner of the woodshed for / its dregs and dreck: tools with no handle, / ten candle-ends not worth a candle, / old lumber banished from the Temple. . . ." But the "dead wood of dry verse" in need of renewal in the old third stanza; and the "wake of refuse, dacron rope," of the implicitly wooden yachts of stanza four; the dark wood of stanza five; the stacked birch of stanza six; the "Bible chopped and crucified" of stanza seven; and, least and most interesting, the old china doorknobs of stanza nine—all develop into the same *pot pourri*:

(4) *Fierce, fireless mind, running down hill.*
   Look up and see the harbor fill:
   business as usual in eclipse
   goes down to the sea in ships—
   wake of refuse, dacron rope,
   bound for Bermuda or Good Hope,
   all bright before the morning watch
   the wine dark hulls of yawl and ketch.

(5) *I watch a glass of water wet*
   with a fine fuzz of icy sweat,
   silvery colors touched with sky,
   serene in their neutrality—
   yet if I shift, or change my mood,
   I see some object made of wood,
   background behind it of brown grain,
   to darken it, but not to stain.

(6) *Oh that the spirit could remain*
   tinged but untarnished by its strain!
   Better dressed and stacking birch,
   or lost with the Faithful at Church—
   Oh anywhere, but somewhere else!
   And now the new electric bells,
   clearly chiming, "Faith of our fathers,"
   and now the congregation gathers.

(7) *O Bible chopped and crucified*
   in hymns we hear but do not read,
   none of the milder subtleties
   of grace or art will sweeten these
   stiff quatrains shovelled out four-square—
   they sing of peace, and preach despair;
   yet they gave darkness some control,
   and left a loophole for the soul.

(8) No, put old clothes on, and explore
     the corners of the woodshed for
     its dregs and dreck: tools with no handle,
     ten candle-ends not worth a candle,
     old lumber banished from the Temple,
     damned by Paul's precept and example,
     cast from the kingdom, banned in Israel,
     the wordless sign, the tinkling cymbal.

(9) When will we see Him face to face?
     Each day, He shines through darker glass.
     In this small town where everything
     is known, I see His vanishing
     emblems, His white spire and flag-
     pole sticking out above the fog,
     like old white china doorknobs, sad,
     slight, useless things to calm the mad. (NO)

The ninth stanza, like the third, was considerably revised. In
both revisions, the presence of the poet is concealed. In the
third stanza, as we saw, small "creatures of the night" replaced
the person of the poet. In the ninth stanza, God Himself does.
Here is the original version of the ninth stanza:

> Empty, irresolute, ashamed,
> when the sacred texts are named,
> I lie here on my bed apart,
> and when I look into my heart,
> I discover none of the great
> subjects: death, friendship, love and hate—
> only old china doorknobs, sad,
> slight, useless things to calm the mad.[5]

The pot pourri is his own mind—or else his heart, as Yeats's
poem would have it. Either way, it is the vessel of all creation.
And to epitomize Lowell's new "foul rag-and-bone shop," the
"old china doorknobs" are a telling detail. Their prototype, and
rationale, may be found in the "Skunk Hour" symposium,
toward the end of Lowell's comment on that poem: "I began to
feel that real poetry came, not from fierce confessions, but from
something almost meaningless but imagined. I was haunted by
an image of a blue china doorknob. I never used the doorknob,

5. *Ibid.*

or knew what it meant, yet somehow it started the current of images in my opening stanzas."[6] The old china doorknobs in "Waking Early Sunday Morning," together with all the "dregs and dreck" of the first nine stanzas, correspond to the current of images in the opening stanzas of "Skunk Hour"; they give their poem, in Lowell's words, "an earth to stand on, and space to breathe." The junk heap is "almost meaningless but imagined."

That the china doorknobs are only "sad, / slight useless things to calm the mad" is therefore nothing against them—as Oscar Wilde and Susan Sontag have explained: "It was Wilde who formulated an important element of the Camp sensibility—the equivalence of all objects—when he announced his intention of 'living up' to his blue-and-white china, or declared that a doorknob could be as admirable as a painting."[7] The "equivalence of all objects" is the key to the here and now, and to the correspondence of Lowell's "woodshed" with Yeats's "rag-and-bone shop," as the locus or vessel of the poet's creative night.

But Lowell's poem is even more ambitious than Yeats's. Its scope is considerably wider. "Waking Early Sunday Morning" moves between the personal and the global. The poet's own creative need for renewal and the mortal need of his country and the globe are conflated by the poem's breathing movement, the mind's expansion and contraction between the two. To the pot pourri of his mind, as the vessel of creation, he adds "a million foreskins stacked like trash," in a Scriptural figure that doubles for current events:

(10)   *Hammering military splendor,*
     top-heavy Goliath in full armor—
     little redemption in the mass
     liquidations of their brass,
     elephant and phalanx moving
     with the times and still improving,
     when that kingdom hit the crash:
     a million foreskins stacked like trash . . .

6. Lowell, in the symposium "On Robert Lowell's 'Skunk Hour,' " in Anthony Ostroff (ed.), *The Contemporary Poet as Artist and Critic: Eight Symposia* (Boston: Little, Brown & Company, 1964), pp. 109–10.

7. Susan Sontag, "Notes on 'Camp,' " in *Against Interpretation and Other Essays* (New York: Farrar, Straus & Giroux, 1966), p. 289.

(11) *Sing softer! But what if a new*
      diminuendo brings no true
      tenderness, only restlessness,
      excess, the hunger for success,
      sanity of self-deception
      fixed and kicked by reckless caution,
      while we listen to the bells—
      anywhere, but somewhere else! (NO)

Then, in the twelfth stanza, repeating the phrase with which
the poem opens, the poem reaches a climax of lyric, personal
candor:

> *O to break loose. All life's grandeur*
> *is something with a girl in summer . . . ,*

where the juxtaposition and contrast of "all life's grandeur"
with the simplicity of "a girl in summer" is both surprised and
approved by the rhyme. Extremes of high and low, and of
permanence and transience, here meet, with the contents of a
lifetime reduced to the span of a summer, and human aspira-
tion to a nameless affair. At this peak of disclosure the figure of
the poet passes into the figure of the president, unclothed:

(12) *O to break loose. All life's grandeur*
      is something with a girl in summer . . .
      elated as the President
      girdled by his establishment
      this Sunday morning, free to chaff
      his own thoughts with his bear-cuffed staff,
      swimming nude, unbuttoned, sick
      of his ghost-written rhetoric! (NO)

The need for renewal is both personal and national. The president's establishment is as constricting as a woman's girdle; there
is a momentary echo of the meaning as well as the sound of
"girl" in "girdle": he is made womanish by wearing it; he needs
to break loose, to thresh his own thoughts; he does thresh or
"cuff" his staff, who are "bear-cuffed" in other ways, too: they
are held captive, like trained bears, and they are buffeted by the
Russian bear, as well as by their own bear-like president. The
president (Lyndon B. Johnson) is bear-like in that he is human

and gross, gross as some Roman emperor in his bath[8] and heavy as the bear of Delmore Schwartz:

> The heavy bear who goes with me,
> A manifold honey to smear his face,
> Clumsy and lumbering here and there,
> The central ton of every place,
> The hungry beating brutish one
> In love with candy, anger, and sleep,
> Crazy factotum, dishevelling all,
> Climbs the building, kicks the football,
> Boxes his brother in the hate-ridden city.[9]

Schwartz's heavy bear is Lowell's monster, too, and his basis for conflating himself with the president:

> That inescapable animal walks with me,
> Has followed me since the black womb held. . . .
> Stretches to embrace the very dear
> With whom I would walk without him near,
> Touches her grossly, although a word
> Would bare my heart and make me clear. . . .[10]

Clear as the glass of water in Lowell's fifth stanza. Lowell bares his heart in the phrase "something with a girl in summer," and, more grandly, in the figure of the president bare. All that is human swims there, with the salmon. And the whole transaction is conducted through the stanza of "The Garden."

8. "The theme that connects my translations is Rome, the greatness and horror of her Empire," writes Lowell in a note at the beginning of *Near the Ocean.* The two halves of the book—the original poems and the imitations of continental poets—hinge upon the theme of Rome's decline and "The Ruins of Time." The title *Near the Ocean* suggests the imminence of the final ruin. At the mouth of the Hudson, ice melts into the sea.

Daniel Hoffman's essay-review, "Robert Lowell's *Near the Ocean:* The Greatness and Horror of Empire," in the *Hollins Critic,* IV (February, 1967), 1–16, emphasizes the ambition and scope of that volume (and indeed of Lowell's work as a whole), and draws attention to its governing parallel between Rome and modern America.

9. Delmore Schwartz, "The Heavy Bear Who Goes with Me," in *Summer Knowledge: New and Selected Poems 1938–1958* (Garden City, N.Y.: Doubleday & Company, 1959), pp. 74–75.

10. *Ibid.*

(13) No weekends for the gods now. Wars
     flicker, earth licks its open sores,
     fresh breakage, fresh promotions, chance
     assassinations, no advance.
     Only man thinning out his kind
     sounds through the Sabbath noon, the blind
     swipe of the pruner and his knife
     busy about the tree of life . . . (NO)

The recollection of Marvell's pastoral, "Annihilating all that's
made / To a green Thought in a green Shade," moves in hectic
contrast here.

(14) Pity the planet, all joy gone
     from this sweet volcanic cone;
     peace to our children when they fall
     in small war on the heels of small
     war—until the end of time
     to police the earth, a ghost
     orbiting forever lost
     in our monotonous sublime. (NO)

Stanzas ten to fourteen, then, continue the figure of the first
nine stanzas, but with the personal expanding into national and
global dimensions; the figure of the poet (in disclosure) becomes the figure of the entire nation, conspicuously in the
person of the president, who is bare (or disclosed) and even
Russian bear-like in his monstrous truth: "unbuttoned, sick / of
his ghost-written rhetoric!" The poem as a whole illustrates
Auerbach's figura: "Figural interpretation establishes a connection between two events or persons, the first of which signifies
not only itself but also the second, while the second encompas-
ses and fulfills the first. The two poles of the figure are separate
in time, but both, being real events or figures, are within time,
within the stream of historical life."[11] Lowell has escaped the
ivory tower and jumped—but as a poet—into Auerbach's
"stream of historical life."

I have already mentioned my admiration for the amazing
candor of the pivotal couplet, which in itself joins the ampli-

11. Erich Auerbach, "Figura" (1944), in Scenes from the Drama of
European Literature: Six Essays (New York: Meridian Books, 1959), p.
53.

tude of "all life's grandeur" to the minute intimacy of "something with a girl in summer." With it, the poem jumps into the pool of the president nude: from the sublime to the ridiculous, and back and forth. The lyrical and the political, intimacy and publicity oscillate, like alternating current, or like Shakespeare's *Antony and Cleopatra*; and history and poetry are joined. The *movement* makes the enabling field of renewal. The desolation and mockery of the poem's concluding image (the "sweet volcanic cone") constantly renew the lyric truth. Its tragic implications make its strength—its strength to imagine nearly hopeless negation in actual fact.

So history and poetry validate each other. As image and idea, material and form, or other poles of meaning or perception they contrast; the comprehending movement makes them new, perceives them newly—the military trash and the private lumber in one junk heap. The representation of form or style, which the unpromising material moves against, as anti-style, is the stanza form. Lowell borrows the stanza of Marvell's "Garden," and loads it with china doorknobs, dacron rope and a million severed foreskins, trophies all. He remembers the happy garden of the world. The stanza of the foreskins, stanza ten, with its image of the Goliath brought to earth, figures after Toynbee the American courtship of destruction. Toynbee, in a section on "The Suicidalness of Militarism" uses Goliath as a figure for the militarist pursuit of disaster, and discovers in the fate of Assyria an example of suicide.[12]

"The disaster in which the Assyrian military power met its end in 614–610 B.C. was one of the completest yet known to history. It involved not only the destruction of the Assyrian war-machine but also the extinction of the Assyrian state and the extermination of the Assyrian people," he begins—proceeding to study the events that led up to their extermination. "The Assyrian war-machine . . . was continuously overhauled, reno-

12. Arnold J. Toynbee, *A Study of History*, Abridgment of Vols. I–VI, by D. C. Somervell (New York: Oxford University Press, 1947), pp. 336–43.

Mr. Lowell wrote to me, ". . . the Assyrian passage in Toynbee was just what I had in mind, tho I had forgotten about his using Goliath. . . ." (Letter dated June 13, 1967.)

vated and reinforced right down to the day of its destruction."[13] But, as Lowell puts it, there was "little redemption in the mass / liquidations of their brass, / elephant and phalanx moving / with the times and still improving. . . ." Toynbee: "Behind the facade of her military triumphs, Assyria had been engaged in committing slow suicide."[14] Is this not "man's lovely, / peculiar power to choose life and die—" that we learned about from Yankee Colonel Shaw?

Lowell's "hammering military splendor, / top-heavy Goliath in full armor—" finds a harrowing prototype in Toynbee's account:

. . . The indomitable warrior who stood at bay in the breach at Nineveh in 612 was 'a corpse in armour,' whose frame was only held erect by the massiveness of the military accountrements in which this *felo de se* had smothered himself to death. When the Median and Babylonian storming party reached the stiff and menacing figure and sent it clattering and crashing down the moraine of ruined brickwork into the fosse below, they did not suspect that their terrible adversary was no longer a living man at the moment when they struck their daring, and apparently decisive, blow.[15]

"When that kingdom hit the crash: / a million foreskins stacked like trash. . . ." The cycles of history repeat their heartless negations.

> Back and forth!
> Back and forth, back and forth—
> my one point of rest
> is the orange and black
> oriole's swinging nest! (*FUD*)

The one certainty, it seems, is the certainty of animal flux. The stanza that concludes "Waking Early Sunday Morning" is a mockery of renewal; yet the strength to mock is a stubborn, animal strength, like the strength of the terribly vulnerable skunks. And the monstrous, top-heavy Goliath, like the monster in President Johnson, is brought home, brought into camp, in the poet's self.

13. Toynbee, *Study of History*, p. 338.
14. *Ibid.*, p. 341.
15. *Ibid.*, p. 342.

Robert Lowell is a big man physically. He used to play football. Peter Taylor, who roomed with him at Kenyon, said that the first poem he ever saw by Lowell was written on the back of a sheet of paper diagramming football plays. But he is also noticeably myopic. "It may be," Stanley Kunitz quotes him as saying, "that some people have turned to my poems because of the very things that are wrong with me, I mean the difficulty I have with ordinary living, the impracticability, the myopia."[16] He refers to his myopia in the poem "Eye and Tooth":

> No ease for the boy at the keyhole,
> his telescope,
> when the women's white bodies flashed
> in the bathroom. Young, my eyes began to fail.
> (FUD)

His glasses are such a conspicuous feature of the man that a poster (a very good one) showing them alone, in a greatly enlarged photograph, was used to advertise one of his readings. It happened to be the reading (at the University of Virginia, February 22, 1968) at which he was introduced by Peter Taylor's reminiscence of his football days. The incongruity of the athletics and the myopia was appropriate. Lowell tends to think of his body as if it were Delmore Schwartz's heavy bear.

But the figural identification of Lowell's monster with himself is a strenuous endeavor—and throughout his work it makes an obsessive theme. The Cain inhabiting Lambkin, in *Lord Weary's Castle*; "The Fat Man in the Mirror," in *The Mills of the Kavanaughs*; the "skirt-mad Mussolini" of "Beyond the Alps," in *Life Studies* ("He was one of us / only, pure prose"); the Stalin of "To Delmore Schwartz," in the same volume; and finally the monsters of "Florence" ("Pity the monsters!") and "Caligula" ("my lowest depths of possibility"), in the volume *For the Union Dead*—are some examples. Lowell's monster is at least an honest devil.

Countering the unlovely material with great formality and in a work of love ("It is a paradox that poetry has to be a technical act, of extreme difficulty, when it wants only to know the

16. Stanley Kunitz, "Telling the Time," *Salmagundi*, I, 4 (1966–67), 23.

untechnical homely fulness of the world," wrote John Crowe Ransom in *The World's Body*[17]), Lowell has cast a whole trilogy of poems in the stanza of Marvell's "The Garden." The other two poems—after "Waking Early Sunday Morning"—are "Fourth of July in Maine" and the title poem of the sequence, "Near the Ocean." Lowell called it a trilogy when he read it for the Academy of American Poets in the spring of 1966. For variety, however, he read with it two additional poems, which are not in the stanza of "The Garden," inserting them between the second and third parts. He has kept this five-part arrangement, calling the whole pentad "Near the Ocean" in the 1967 volume. Since the two additional poems, "The Opposite House" and "Central Park," have already been discussed in the preceding chapter, I will focus now on the trilogy itself, as the principal feature of the volume.[18]

It is relevant, however, that the poems Lowell uses to break the monotony are city poems. The poems in the stanza-form of "The Garden" have the rural setting of a Maine coastal town, Castine, where Mr. Lowell spends his summers, though the last of these poems contains a stanza about New York City. The five poems accordingly enact the following pattern: country, country, city, city, country. The dialectical movement of the pattern justifies keeping the five-part arrangement. The alterna-

17. John Crowe Ransom, *The World's Body* (New York: Charles Scribner's Sons, 1938), p. xi.

18. Daniel Hoffman refers to the poems of the trilogy as "the three principal poems in the first half of his new book: 'Waking Early Sunday Morning,' 'Fourth of July in Castine [sic],' and the title poem." (Hoffman, "Robert Lowell's *Near the Ocean*," p. 15.) G. S. Fraser, on the other hand, does not select the trilogy for emphasis. Professor Fraser describes the book as follows: "Robert Lowell's new volume divides into two almost equal halves. The first half consists of original poems, scenic ruminations set in Maine or New York City, poems to persons, and a fine short elegy for Theodore Roethke. The second half consists of translations from Juvenal and Horace, from the most famous canto of Dante's 'Inferno,' and from the Spanish Renaissance poets, Quevedo and Gongora, dealing with the theme of the ruins of time, the war between transience and permanence. The two halves of the book reinforce each other, expressing a similar mood of creative disillusionment and half-reluctant zest." ("Unmonotonous Sublime" [review of Robert Lowell's *Near the Ocean*], *The New York Times Book Review* [January 15, 1967], 6.)

tion between the regions contains a reflection of the poet's life and at the same time even suggests sonata form, with its recapitulation of both themes in the concluding section.

"Fourth of July in Maine," the second poem in the sequence, continues the movement we saw in "Waking Early Sunday Morning," between the public and the private—between the national and global predicament, on the one hand, and the private or personal need, on the other. It is seventeen stanzas long. But something of an epitome of the whole poem may be found in stanzas eleven through thirteen, about Lowell's only daughter, Harriet, aged ten and a half, and some guinea pigs she kept as pets. Harriet is named after Harriet Winslow, to whom the poem is dedicated. In "Soft Wood," in *For the Union Dead*, Harriet Winslow is the cousin who "was more to me than my mother." The "soft wood" is the vulnerable material of the house, in that poem and in this one, "this white Colonial frame house, / willed downward, Dear, from you to us" (NO). "Fourth of July in Maine" celebrates the house, in all of the lovable vulnerability of its "soft wood," and with all of its implications of the family line, as well as of the nation and the human race. This tenderness, and a reminiscence of Yeats's "A Prayer for my Daughter," are contained in the stanzas devoted to the daughter and her guinea pigs:

> Blue-ribboned, blue-jeaned, named for you,
> our daughter cartwheels on the blue—
> may your proportion strengthen her
> to live through the millennial year
> Two Thousand, and like you possess
> friends, independence, and a house,
> herself God's plenty, mistress of
> your tireless sedentary love.
>
> Her two angora guinea pigs
> are nibbling seed, the news, and twigs—
> untroubled, petrified, atremble,
> a mother and her daughter, so humble,
> giving, idle and sensitive,
> few animals will let them live,
> and only a vegetarian God
> could look on them and call them good.

> Man's poorest cousins, harmonies
> of lust and appetite and ease,
> little pacific things, who graze
> the grass about their box, they praise
> whatever stupor gave them breath
> to multiply before their death—
> Evolution's snails, by birth,
> outrunning man who runs the earth. (NO)

The tone and diction with which the cousin is addressed, in the first of these stanzas, might have suited Yeats for Lady Gregory. From that peak of ceremony and "God's plenty," to the trough of the lustful guinea pigs, "Man's poorest cousins," is a fall that spans the extremes of human possibility. A tenderness toward the guinea pigs is validated by humor: "only a vegetarian God / could look at them and call them good." (But "Words for a Guinea Pig," in the *Notebook*, do not evoke sympathy: " 'They will paint me like Cromwell with all my warts: / small mop with a tumor and eyes too popped for thought; / I was a rhinoceros when jumped by my sons. / I ate and bred, and then I only ate. . . .' ") ". . . Outrunning man who runs the earth," they have the vigor but not the beauty of the skunks in "Skunk Hour." Harriet's guinea pigs "praise / whatever stupor gave them breath / to multiply before their death—" just as in "Waking Early Sunday Morning" the salmon, serving also as an image of man, "clear the top on the last try, / alive enough to spawn and die." It is not a self-flattering image. It is only authentic.

But the endeavor to face the authentic image requires daily renewal. The image is one of intolerable flux; but it is suicide to evade it or repress it. The nation's inability to break loose, to gain independence from its blind, suicidal conservatism, is the subject of this Independence Day poem. The nation's need is figured, in the final stanza, in the personal need to face the detail of flux: the quotidian "household fire." Here are the poem's first two and last two stanzas:

> Another summer! Our Independence
> Day Parade, all innocence
> of children's costumes, helps resist
> the communist and socialist.

Five nations: Dutch, French, Englishmen,
Indians, and we, who held Castine,
rise from their graves in combat gear—
world-losers elsewhere, conquerors here!

Civil Rights clergy face again
the scions of the good old strain,
the poor who always must remain
poor and Republicans in Maine,
upholders of the American Dream,
who will not sink and cannot swim—
O Emersonian self-reliance,
O lethargy of Russian peasants!

. . . .

Far off that time of gentleness,
when man, still licensed to increase,
unfallen and unmated, heard
only the uncreated Word—
when God the Logos still had wit
to hide his bloody hands, and sit
in silence, while his peace was sung.
Then the universe was young.

We watch the logs fall. Fire once gone,
we're done for: we escape the sun,
rising and setting, a red coal,
until it cinders like the soul.
Great ash and sun of freedom, give
us this day the warmth to live,
and face the household fire. We turn
our backs, and feel the whiskey burn. (NO)

The juxtaposition of the Logos and the logs and the conflation of Gemütlichkeit with astronomy measure the scope and movement of this poem.

The title poem of the trilogy, "Near the Ocean," comes to just eight stanzas. It is marked "For E. H. L.," the poet's wife. The poem is intensely personal and still prophetic, ranging across all history with a lover's mind.[19] "The house," the theatre of the world, is the tragic stage:

19. Richard Poirier calls Robert Lowell "our truest historian": "More than any contemporary writer, poet or novelist, Lowell has created the

> The house is filled. The last heartthrob
> thrills through her flesh. The hero stands,
> stunned by the applauding hands,
> and lifts her head to please the mob . . .
> No, young and starry-eyed, the brother
> and sister wait before their mother,
> old iron-bruises, powder, "Child,
> these breasts . . ." He knows. And if she's killed
>
> his treadmill heart will never rest—
> his wet mouth pressed to some slack breast,
> or shifting over on his back . . .
> The severed radiance filters back,
> athirst for nightlife—gorgon head,
> fished up from the Aegean dead,
> with all its stranded snakes uncoiled,
> here beheaded and despoiled. (NO)

The quoted words are Clytaemestra's to Orestes, spoken to him when he is about to kill her. "And if she's killed / his treadmill heart will never rest— / his wet mouth pressed to some slack breast," as in the satanic "Going to and fro." The gorgon head, here as in the earlier poem, "Florence," is a figure of the intolerable flux. To cut it off is to deny the grisly affair—and to repeat a cycle. It is an ancient, an archetypal, human story:

> We hear the ocean. Older seas
> and deserts give asylum, peace
> to each abortion and mistake.
> Lost in the Near Eastern dreck,
> the tyrant and tyrannicide
> lie like the bridegroom and the bride;
> the battering ram, abandoned, prone,
> beside the ape-man's phallic stone.

---

language, cool and violent all at once, of contemporary introspection. He is our truest historian. He evokes the past not as if it alone were history but as if its meaning exists necessarily in its relation to that more imporant element of history which is himself, now and here; and he confronts literature, as he does in *Imitations*, not, again, as something that belongs to the past but that belongs to him, taking in him some special shape which can then be given to us." (Richard Poirier, "Our Truest Historian" [review of *For the Union Dead*], *Book Week*, II [Oct. 11, 1964], 16. I am indebted to Mark Schorer for this reference.)

Betrayals! Was it the first night?
They stood against a black and white
inland New England backdrop. No dogs
there, horse or hunter, only frogs
chirring from the dark trees and swamps.
Elms watching like extinguished lamps.
Knee-high hedges of black sheep
encircling them at every step. (NO)

The story is this: love and promiscuity and betrayal, cycles as ancient and sordid as the *Oresteia's*; rising, like some yeast, in their "simmer of rot and renewal"; falling short of the comprehending whole, the sex of the ocean.

Some subway-green coldwater flat,
its walls tattooed with neon light,
then high delirious squalor, food
burned down with vodka . . . menstrual blood
caking the covers, when they woke
to the dry, childless Sunday walk,
saw cars on Brooklyn Bridge descend
through steel and coal dust to land's end.

. . . .

Is it this shore? Their eyes worn white
as moons from hitting bottom? Night,
the sandfleas scissoring their feet,
the sandbed cooling to concrete,
one borrowed blanket, lights of cars
shining down at them like stars? . . .
Sand built the lost Atlantis . . . sand,
Atlantic ocean, condoms, sand. (NO)

The flux of ocean and sand—all creation, all destruction—condoms, lovers, and stars are here, centered in a particular mind's simmer of disillusionment and awareness. Given the traction of private, personal experience, the realization of universal process can possibly be shared. Here in a single man's relived remorse—relived, cast out on the stage of the imagination—the monstrous promiscuity and betrayal of a lifetime live in an authentic flux of life-and-death. " 'In the destructive element immerse,' " said Conrad's Stein; acceptance of the flux is liberation—as in the "Epigram" for Hannah Arendt:

> Think of Leonidas perhaps and the hoplites
> glittering with liberation,
> as they combed one another's golden Botticellian
> hair at Thermopylae—friends and lovers,
> the bride and the bridegroom—
> and moved into position to die. (FUD)

"Near the Ocean" culminates in a lyric acceptance of annihilation. The gallows-whimsy of Wallace Stevens, in "Lebensweisheitspielerei," offers a comparable discovery:

> Each person completely touches us
> With what he is and as he is,
> In the stale grandeur of annihilation.

In Lowell's concluding stanza the stale grandeur of the total past is annihilated in a moment of candor, a moment out of time, when the thought of his wife, Elizabeth, beside him, moves him with tenderness and terror at once, moves him to accept the way things are:

> Sleep, sleep. The ocean, grinding stones,
> can only speak the present tense;
> nothing will age, nothing will last,
> or take corruption from the past.

("Both past and future are created by and proceed from that which is perpetually present . . . , eternity, which stands still and is neither past nor future," wrote Saint Augustine in his Confessions.)

> A hand, your hand then! I'm afraid
> to touch the crisp hair on your head—
> Monster loved for what you are,
> till time, that buries us, lay bare. (NO)

The comprehension of the self in the monster, here and now, alone affords progress and renewal and release.

~~~~~~~~~~~~~~~

The rest is silence. The alternation of the mind, the reader's mind, between the classical tragedy of the Oresteia and a particular modern life, bridging at the same time the tenderness and terror implicit in both, corresponds to the mysterious jump from Rome to America of which Lowell speaks. In a note prefacing the volume *Near the Ocean,* he remarks: "The theme that connects my translations is Rome, the greatness and horror of her Empire. . . . How one jumps from Rome to the America of my own poems is something of a mystery to me. Perhaps the bridge is made by the brilliant drawings of Sidney Nolan. May my lines throw some light on his!" Although this can be read as a light and graceful tribute to the artist, the mystery of which Lowell speaks can be genuinely dark. For the resolution of the poems comes only in silence. Opposite or contrasting perspectives generate movement, the heuristic movement of the mind as it vacillates between the poem's extremes. The poem is comprehended, as an equilibrium of conflicting voices, by the silence. Dialectical alternation between the words and their particular silence, something like the movement of Hegelian opposites, constitutes the principle of lyric ambivalence.

This is the movement Yeats observed in the scheme of his interpenetrating gyres. It is fundamental to consciousness itself. Organized in the polarity of a poem, it is the way the poem makes itself felt. In Lowell it begins to dissolve the rigid duality of life and art, and to bear historical witness in aesthetic form. The body of Lowell's poems is the world's body. Abandoning the pretense that art must be a preservative, and comprehending the movement of life in death, Lowell's work serves to make it new.

❧ VIII. LOWELL'S NOTEBOOK

One wants words meat-hooked from the living steer. . . .
ROBERT LOWELL

❧ Originally, at readings, Lowell referred to it as the *Notebook of a Year;* later it became *Notebook 1967–68.* "Notebook," in both titles, is very casual—and the later title, besides being casual, is harder, crisper, more prosaic or journalistic or historic, and less inclined to announce its connections with myth.

The connections, of course, are there. The venerable and mythy antiquity of seasonal recurrence, in the round of the year, can be taken as axiomatic; and its periodic secularization, as by the offhand, familiar, casual style suggested by both titles but especially by the later one, is a corollary of the sacred character of the year. Another modern instance of the secular mode may be found in Wordsworth. Early in the *Prelude,* Wordsworth, considering how the animistic presences of nature "Impressed upon all forms the characters / Of danger or desire; and thus did make / The surface of the universal earth . . . / Work like a sea," thought how he might "pursue this theme through every change / Of exercise and play, to which the year / Did summon us in his delightful round." Lowell's *Notebook,* loosely and casually, follows such a round.

The cycle of the *Notebook* is a paradigm of renewal. Renewal of his life, renewal of his work, was the special need that governed the book's inception. The summer after the appearance of *Near the Ocean,* the summer of 1967, began as a dry period for Lowell. But he was stirred, as he remarked in a letter, "to work up my memories and impressions."[1] *Notebook 1967–68*, which appeared almost two summers later, is made up of Lowell's experiences, memories and impressions as they occurred during the cycle of that year, from the summer of 1967 through the following summer. Out of this casual beginning, however, there emerged a new ambition: to consider the *Notebook* as a single, long poem.

The cycle, the circle, the round of the year, provides the plot of the volume as a whole, which Lowell, in the prose "Afterthought," asks to be considered as one poem. It consists of 274 "fourteen line unrhymed blank verse sections," as he describes them. "My plot rolls with the seasons. The separate poems or sections are opportunist and inspired by impulse. Accident threw up subjects, and the plot swallowed them—famished for human chances."

The phrasing consciously echoes a pair of lines in the poem or section "For John Berryman":

> *I feel I know what you have worked through, you*
> *know what I have worked through—these are words. . . .*
> *John, we used the language as if we made it.*
> *Luck threw up the coin, and the plot swallowed,*
> *monster yawning for its mess of pottage.*
> *Ah privacy, as if you wished to mount*
> *some rock by a mossy stream, and count the sheep—*
> *fame that renews the soul, but not the heart.*
> *The ebb tide flings up wonders: rivers, beer-cans,*
> *linguini, bloodstreams; how merrily they gallop*
> *to catch the ocean—Hopkins, Herbert, Thoreau,*
> *born to die like the athletes at early forty—*
> *Abraham lived with less expectancy,*
> *heaven his friend, the earth his follower.* (NBK)

The roiling "wonders" exposed by the ebbing tide of the poet's life (the "rivers, beer-cans, / linguini, bloodstreams; how merrily they gallop / to catch the ocean") are like the "dregs and dreck" in "Waking Early Sunday Morning," or the "sand, / Atlantic ocean, condoms, sand" of "Near the Ocean": they collocate the ephemeral with the oceanic, and both with

1. Robert Lowell, in a letter to me dated June 13, 1967.

the poetic ("how merrily they gallop / to catch the ocean—Hopkins, Herbert, Thoreau, / born to die like the athletes at early forty—"). They discover again the source of human creation in the private place, the intimate self, the individual's personal sincerity; it is the place, once again, "where all the ladders start," as Yeats put it—"in the foul rag-and-bone shop of the heart." ("Ah privacy, as if you wished to mount / some rock by a mossy stream. . . .") The special power of that place may be felt in the paradox observed by Northrop Frye: that the more original an author becomes, the closer he comes to the origin of all literature. Reading John Berryman, Lowell acknowledges the shock of recognition.

Berryman's "dream songs," whose unity is inseparable from the personality or character of Henry, or Berryman's imagined self, are one of the most immediate antecedents of Lowell's *Notebook*. Lowell reviewed 77 *Dream Songs* for the *New York Review*, saying: "In the beginning, Berryman might have grown into an austere, removed poet, but instead he somehow remained deep in the mess of things. . . . With Berryman, each succeeding book is part of a single drive against the barriers of the commonplace"—a remark that might be made of Lowell himself.[2] In the same review he quoted the entire section beginning, "There sat down once, a thing on Henry's heart," and ending:

> But never did Henry, as he thought he did,
> end anyone and hacks her body up
> and hide the pieces, where they may be found.
> He knows: he went over everyone, & nobody's missing.
> Often he reckons, in the dawn, them up.
> Nobody's ever missing.

Lowell commented: "The voice of the man becomes one with the voice of the child here, as their combined rhythm sobs through remorse, wonder and nightmare. It's as if two widely separated parts of a man's life had somehow fused." ("I feel I know what you have worked through, you / know what I have worked through—these are words. . . . / John, we used the

2. Robert Lowell, "The Poetry of John Berryman" (review of 77 *Dream Songs*), *New York Review of Books*, II (May 28, 1964), 3–4.

language as if we made it.") And for the *Harvard Advocate*, after *His Toy, His Dream, His Rest* had appeared, Lowell wrote: "I think *Dream Songs*, now completed, is one of the glories of the age, the single most heroic work in English poetry since the War, since Ezra Pound's *Pisan Cantos*. Berryman handles the language, as if he made it."[3] The repeated assertion underscores the feature that Lowell particularly admired: at the extreme of originality Berryman touches the origin of poetry itself.

But that origin, paradoxically, inward or spiritual though it is, is at the same time, "somehow . . . deep in the mess of things." "Hopkins, Herbert, Thoreau," poets of the immanent, are relevant doubtless for their work's special traction with the earth, as well as for the earthly brevity of their lives. The *Notebook* persistently focuses attention on ephemeral things, and recirculates them through the widest possible context.

For this work of Lowell's there is another contemporary antecedent. Early in the 1950's, the poetry of the mess of things was given a special impetus, at least for Lowell, by Robert Penn Warren. Robert Penn Warren wrote a novel in verse and Lowell reviewed it with enthusiasm, saying that he had read it three times from cover to cover without stopping. It was *Brother to Dragons*, and it came out in 1953, just at the time when Lowell was beginning his long descent from the Alps of his high style.

The metaphor is Lowell's. His poem "Beyond the Alps" opens *Life Studies*; it first appeared in 1953, in the same volume of the *Kenyon Review* that published his review of Warren's *Brother to Dragons*; and Lowell used the metaphor to suggest Warren's achievement: "Warren has written his best book, a big book; he has crossed the Alps and, like Napoleon's shoeless army, has entered the fat, populated riverbottom of the novel."[4]

What exactly does he mean by "the fat, populated riverbottom of the novel"? Since Lowell has evidently reflected some of

---

3. Robert Lowell, in an untitled reply to the editors of *The Harvard Advocate*, CIII (Spring, 1969), 17.
4. Robert Lowell, "Prose Genius in Verse" (review of Robert Penn Warren's *Brother to Dragons*), *Kenyon Review*, XV (1953), 621.

his own achievement and Warren's in the same figurative mirror, the question is worth pursuing. What Lowell particularly likes about Warren's hybrid, he says, is the fact that it is "tactless and voluminous" and yet "also alive." He likes the way it recaptures for poetry some of the ground poetry had ceded to prose. That cession, and its consequence, he describes in the following way:

> . . . Back in the palmy, imperialist days of Victoria, Napoleon's nephew, and Baudelaire, a kind of literary concordat was reached: the ephemeral was ceded to prose. Since then the new poetry has been so scrupulous and electrical, its authors seem seldom to have regretted this Mary and Martha division of labor. Poetry became all that was not prose. Under this dying-to-the-world discipline the stiffest and most matter of fact items were repoeticized—quotations from John of the Cross, usury, statistics, conversations and newspaper clippings. These amazing new poems could absorb everything —everything, that is, except plot and characters, just those things long poems have usually relied upon.[5]

In this context, the sentence about crossing the Alps and entering "the fat, populated riverbottom of the novel" gathers weight: it means rich with ephemera, and inhabited by imaginable people—the ephemeral world in all its fruitful jumble, with three-dimensional characters, and their plot, to organize it. Lowell was excited: "*Brother to Dragons* is a model and an opportunity. It can be imitated without plagiarism, and one hopes its matter and its method will become common property." The opportunity was to recombine poetry with a broader view of life.

Brother to Dragons is a historical novel in verse. Warren wrote in the preface: "Historical sense and poetic sense should not, in the end, be contradictory, for if poetry is the little myth we make, history is the big myth we live, and in our living, constantly remake."[6] For Lowell, the two kinds of sense coalesced in the poetry of *Life Studies*, a poetry that evidently derived from his autobiographical prose. "91 Revere Street," the prose section of *Life Studies*, had been published three years

5. *Ibid.*, p. 620.
6. Robert Penn Warren, *Brother to Dragons, A Tale in Verse and Voices* (New York: Random House, 1953), p. xii.

earlier in *Partisan Review*; and Lowell told Brooks and Warren that "My Last Afternoon with Uncle Devereux Winslow," for example, had been written first in prose. By 1968, his development of the hybrid (or recovery of an original strain) had progressed so far that he could declare flatly, to D. S. Carne-Ross: "I no longer know the difference between prose and verse."[7]

The *Notebook of a Year*, as it was first called—or *Notebook 1967-68*, as it is now called with more resolute historicity—is a further development of the hybrid. On the one hand it is verse. But except for the fourteen-line length of each poem or section, and an iambic pentameter norm, there is no consistently strict measure for the verse; it "often corrupts in single lines to the freedom of prose," writes Lowell in the "Afterthought." On the other hand, the *Notebook* is history. Ostensibly it records the history of a single year as a participant observed it—somewhat as Norman Mailer's book, *Armies of the Night*, records from inside the history of the Pentagon march. Both books are intensely autobiographical and intensely imagined. Mailer goes so far as to subtitle his: *History as a Novel / The Novel as History*. In any case Lowell, a fellow participant, is prominent in it; and "For Norman Mailer" is a poem in Lowell's *Notebook*. Two of the other poems are on the Pentagon march, and —as a further illustration of the political or historical strain in Lowell's book—a whole sequence is devoted to the Chicago convention, which Lowell attended as a companion of Senator McCarthy's.

It is not that political poems, or poems with historical subjects, are being presented as anything new under the sun; but the phenomenal world, or the world of Mailer, the journalist, had become estranged from poetry in the immediate past. Roethke must have been making a similar point, when he said: "There are areas of experience in modern life that simply cannot be rendered by either the formal lyric or straight prose. We need the catalogue in our time. We need the eye close to the object, the poem about the single incident—the animal, the

7. D. S. Carne-Ross, "Conversation with Robert Lowell," *Delos*, I (1968), 166.

child. We must permit poetry to extend consciousness as far, as deeply, as particularly as it can, to recapture, in Stanley Kunitz' phrase, 'what it has lost to some extent to prose.' "[8] Roethke's poem "The Longing" further tells his purpose and shows his task:

> I long for the imperishable quiet at the heart of form. . . .
> In the summer heat, I can smell the dead buffalo,
> The stench of their damp fur drying in the sun,
> The buffalo chips drying.

To extend lyric awareness across the field of prose was the need of the *Notebook*, too. It is not a catalog, but it is a mosaic. Its units focus like the eye close to the object, while the large design is both cumulative and highly disjunctive. It jells finally in the character of the poet as the poem or volume's open, emergent form. The volume or poem as a whole extends awareness, both on the part of the poet and of his reader, "as far, as deeply, as particularly as it can," with the scope of prose but without prose limitations—without the need to dissolve and be understood.

This resistance ("poetry must resist the intelligence almost successfully," according to Wallace Stevens), and something of the grist of prose, may be felt in Lowell's poem "For Theodore Roethke: 1908–1963," as it reappears, revised, in the *Notebook*:

> At Yaddo, you shared a bathroom with a bag
> tree-painter whose boobs bounced in the basin,
> your blues basin where you wished to plunge your head. . . .
> All night, my friend, no friend, you swam my sleep;
> this morning you are lost in the Maine sky,
> close, cold and gray, smoke, smoke-colored cloud.
> Sheeplike, unsociable, reptilian, the shags
> fly in straight lines like duck in a shooting booth,
> divers winning to the darker monochrome.
> You honored nature, helpless, elemental
> creature, and touched the waters of the offing:
> you left them quickened with your name: Ted Roethke. . . .
> Omnipresent, the Mother made you nonexistent,
> you, the ocean's anchor, our high tide. (NBK)

8. Cleanth Brooks and Robert Penn Warren (eds.), *Conversations on the Craft of Poetry* (New York: Holt, Rinehart & Winston, 1961), p. 61.

The opening details are faultlessly observed, nicely presented with suitable diction and kinesthetic effect. But by the end of the poem, what began as a locker-room story reaches us as myth. The "bag / tree-painter whose boobs bounced in the basin, / your blues basin where you wished to plunge your head," has become "Omnipresent, the Mother . . . ," and the vulnerable creatures, the "divers winning to the darker monochrome," are made nonexistent by her Omnipresence. They (with the poet, Ted Roethke) rejoin the oceanic—just as, "Come winter, / Uncle Devereux would blend to the one color" (LS). There is a similar meditation by Wallace Stevens, in "Wild Ducks, People and Distances":

> People might share but never were an element
>
> Like earth and sky. Then he became nothing else
> And they were nothing else. It was late in the year.
> The wild ducks were enveloped.

The principal difference between the *Notebook* version of "For Theodore Roethke" and the version that appeared in *Near the Ocean*, aside from modifications to conform to the semi-sonnet pattern, is the addition of the anecdote about Yaddo. The culminating image is the same: Ted Roethke dead, become the earth itself, the solid globe, concave at ocean bottom, is the "ocean's anchor, our high tide"; but now the pull of gravity makes itself felt by the movement of the earth-mother boobs, as well as by the waters of the ocean. (There are also "earth-mother tits" in Lowell's "At the Green Cabaret," in *Imitations*.) The boobs at the beginning of the poem and the tide at the end respond to each other as alternate reflections of the anchor's mortal gravity.

The name "Yaddo" itself is important primarily because it designates an actual place (the artists' retreat near Saratoga Springs), and it is important for Lowell's poetry to be about real people and actual places. But the name is also, incidentally, interesting for its connotation of shadow on water: the estate was so named because the owner's young daughter had seen a shadow on a pond and called it "yaddo." Water is a governing image in the poem, from the bathroom basin to the ocean floor

—or from the word "Yaddo" to the word "tide." The earthy, ephemeral, irreverent quality of the new opening gives the poem "an earth to stand on, and space to breathe."

The poem, in return, salvages the anecdote, or the experience it records, together with the memory of the man involved, and rescues both from the combustion or forgetfulness that otherwise surely would consume them. The poem transforms the ephemeral. It does so in two ways. It integrates awareness of the ephemeral into awareness of a universal pattern, or an archetype; and it brings the double awareness home into oneself, changes it into the self. This task of transformation is like the task of the *Duino Elegies*, as Rilke describes that in a letter:

> . . . All the forms of the here and now are not merely to be used in a time-limited way, but, so far as we can, instated within those superior significances in which we share. *Not, however, in the Christian sense* (from which I more and more passionately withdraw), but, in a purely mundane, deeply mundane, blissfully mundane consciousness, to instate what is *here* seen and touched within a wider, within the widest orbit—that is what is required. Not within a Beyond, whose shadow darkens the earth, but within a whole, within *the* Whole. . . . Our task is to stamp this provisional, perishing earth into ourselves so deeply, so painfully and passionately, that its being may rise again, "invisibly," in us.[9]

In verse, in the Ninth Elegy, he writes:

> . . . *These things that live on departure*
> *understand when you praise them: fleeting, they look for*
> *rescue through something in us, the most fleeting of all.*
> *Want us to change them entirely, within our invisible hearts,*
> *into—oh, endlessly—into ourselves! Whosoever we are.*

Lowell's revisions for the *Notebook* show him engaged in this task—but, unlike Rilke, with irony to deflate the romantic solemnity. Besides "For Theodore Roethke," consider for example the poem that follows it in the volume *Near the Ocean*, "1958." The latter also reappears, somewhat changed, in the *Notebook*. The new version is made more personal, and more

---

9. Rainer Maria Rilke, *Duino Elegies*, trans. J. B. Leishman and Stephen Spender (New York: W. W. Norton & Company, 1939), p. 128.

dramatic, by two touches: the naming of Ann Adden, and Lowell's self-interruption in line ten: "a rose—not there, a week earlier! We stand. . . ." His own personality breaks in, makes us even more aware of his presence, his autobiographical presence, countering but also increasing the weight of myth, the transformation of a memory into what Rilke has called the "vibration spheres of the universe," at the same time that the whole is handled with humor:

> Remember standing with me in the dark,
> Ann Adden? In the wild house? Everything—
> I mad, you mad for me? And brought my ring,
> that twelve-carat lunk of gold there . . . my Joan of Arc,
> undeviating then from the true mark—
> robust, ah taciturn! Remember our playing
> Marian Anderson in Mozart's Shepherd King,
> Il Re Pastore there? O Hammerheaded Shark,
> the Rainbow Salmon of the World, your hand
> a rose—not there, a week earlier! we stand. . . .
> We ski-walked the eggshell at the Mittersill,
> Pascal's infinite, perfect, fearful sphere—
> the border nowhere, your center everywhere. . . .
> And if I forget you, Ann, may my right hand . . . (NBK)

The "Rainbow Salmon of the World" recalls the rainbow of "The Quaker Graveyard," where "The Lord survives the rainbow of His will" (LWC), in a metaphor for the terrible changeableness of things, in a world where the monster Leviathan is victim, and gentle Quakers ungently "hack the coiling life out," and terror reaches even "Our Lady of Walsingham," whose face, "Expressionless, expresses God," the God of the spatial silences that terrified Pascal. And the Salmon recalls "Waking Early Sunday Morning," the "chinook / salmon" of cyclic generation in the animal kingdom, whose subjects, by necessity, we are.

But all this is handled with a touch of humor, a humorous irony that becomes apparent, in the *Notebook*, in the context of the next poem, "1968." This poem, naming a perspective ten years more mature, was evidently made of prose sentences taken from an actual letter. The letter is from the Isolde of the earlier poem; the interval has turned her into a matron.

> "Dear Lowell, sitting sixty feet above the sea,
> hearing my father build a house on this cliff,
> sixty feet above the Penobscot Bay,
> returning here from my ten years in Europe,
> waiting for emigration papers, work cards etc.;
> I chanced to read your book, Near the Ocean.
> I'm older . . . an extending potency. . . .
> What I'd like to say is humanity,
> like the breezy Pharaohs the first Egyptians sculpted.
> What I write to tell you is what a shining
> remembrance of someone, of you, to hold of . . . me—
> I aggrandize. . . . 1958; now thundered
> all the way through to that seemingly virginal time,
> I fled America. We have a Viking son of three." (NBK)

The pair of poems is collectively titled, with unmistakable though mixed irony, "Mania."

The effect of deliberately breaking artistic illusion, to assert historical or autobiographical awareness, is similarly achieved by the very insertion of poems from the earlier books into the new cycle. That this is a common practice does not alter the effect. Each time a poet revises a poem in public, the spell of the finished surface is for a moment broken; readers are taken behind the scenes, or into the artist's workshop, by the very awareness that this is an act of revision. "Familiar Quotations (For Harriet)," for example, is a deliberate pastiche of lines from Lowell's earlier poems; and his insertion of "In the Cage," with the explicit marking, "Winter 1944 [from Lord Weary's Castle]," into the Notebook as the poem following "Rats," reminds the reader overtly of the author's corpus, and calls attention to its autobiographical drift.

"Rats" begins with a memory of "the Danbury Jail," the federal penitentiary in Danbury, Connecticut, where Lowell served part of his sentence for the felony of refusing to obey the draft; it develops into an acrid comparison of rats and men:

> A friend of that day, the Black Muslim
> on our masons' gang at the Danbury Jail,
> held his hand over the postcard Connecticut
> landscape, scarred by us and a few mean human houses,
> saying, "Only man is miserable."

He was wrong though, he forgot the rats. A pair
in an enclosure kills the rest, then breeds a clan.
Stranger rats with their wrong clan-smell stumble
on the clan, are run squeaking with tails and backs split open
up trees and fences—to die of nervous shock.
Someone rigged the enclosure with electric levers
that could give the rats an orgasm. Soon the rats learned
to press the levers, did nothing else—still on the trip,
they died of starvation in a litter of food. (NBK)

"In the Cage," a quarter of a century old, is placed after
"Rats" in connection with the same jail experience. Only a
clause is changed in the reprinting: "and age / Blackens the
heart of Adam" becomes "the age / numbs the failed nerve to
service." But in the earlier poem the autobiographical element
had been more artfully distanced. The new collocation, with
the reference to Danbury in "Rats," breaks the illusion of that
distance; and the revised phrase, "the failed nerve," more
openly acknowledges an accusation of cowardice. Ironic ambigu-
ities in the word "service" (armed service, which he had refused, or prison-term service, which he accepted instead) more
than compensate, however, for whatever was lost in the loss of
the reference to Adam. The new poem is paradoxically both
more artful and more autobiographical in the same stroke.

Behind the breaking and re-establishing of illusion, behind
the artifice of the autobiographical awareness, and implicit in
the equation of the life with the writing, of the body of the poet
with the corpus of his work ("this open book . . . my open
coffin"), is the figure of the circle. The Notebook is bound by
the circle of a year, and its parts reflect corresponding cycles of
all sorts: the "invisible / coronary," crowning and circular net-
work of the bloodstream; the cycles of the earth's waters,
through the rivers, to the ocean, and back again across the sky;
the paths of the stars; the cycles of human and animal conflict
and generation, mindful and mindless, mythic and historical;
the pattern of the seasons, the year. These are not the subjects
of the poems, but implicit and traditional clues to their coherence. The awareness of their fabric brings together, in a single
thought, poetry, "the little myth we make," and history, "the

big myth we live, and in our living, constantly remake." Not only is there no contradiction; poetry and history validate each other.

"Che Guevara," for example, is a response to the week of news about the hunting down and killing, in Bolivia, of that political figure. Guevara, some years after his success in the Cuban revolution, was leading a guerilla band through the Bolivian jungle, trying to foment revolution among the peasants or underprivileged there, and eventually throughout the rest of Latin America. But Yankee agents helped the Bolivian soldiers track him down, capture him and shoot him. "Our clasped, illicit hands," in Lowell's response, by evoking an image of the poet clandestine with a girl, gives traction to his sense of complicity in the killing of Che, and in the oppression of the poor whose cause Che espoused, and in criminality of every sort, as a descendant of Cain, a felon, a fellow of Czar Lepke's and Emperor Caligula's, as well as of "the outlaw" in this poem:

> Week of Che Guevara, hunted, hurt,
> held prisoner one lost day, then gangstered down
> for gold, for justice—violence cracking on violence,
> rock on rock, the corpse of the last armed prophet
> laid out on a sink in a shed, displayed by flashlight—
> as the leaves light up, still green, this afternoon,
> and burn to frittered reds; as the oak, branch-lopped
> to go on living, swells with goiters like a fruit-tree,
> as the sides of the high white stone buildings over-
> shadow the poor, too new for the new world,
> Manhattan, where our clasped, illicit hands
> pulse, stop the bloodstream as if it hit rock. . . .
> Rest for the outlaw . . . kings once hid in oaks,
> with prices on their heads, and watched for game. (NBK)

The kings in the last two lines include both the historical Charles II, who actually hid in an oak, in the month of September, and the mythical kings and year-gods of Frazer's *Golden Bough*, whose pattern of death and rebirth enacts the cyclic renewal of the seasons. Man and beast are once again compared, as hunter and hunted, archetypal pair, in Lowell's image of the killing; and the *lex talionis* rules as hard as rock.

The tone is perfectly ambivalent, perfectly mixed: neither tribute nor disapproval asserts dominion. When the poem was published in a collection called ¡Viva Che! *Contributions in Tribute to Ernesto "Che" Guevara* (London, 1968), Lowell added a note disclaiming polemics: "This is what it is, and no more a tribute to Che than Shakespeare's Hotspur is a tribute."[10] Characteristically, the disclaimer itself is somewhat ambivalent.

In the *Notebook*, "Che Guevara" is followed by a poem called "Caracas," then by the two poems on the Pentagon march, in which Lowell participated, in opposition to the established order, though evidently without rancor: "Health to those who held, / health to the green steel head . . ." They, in turn, are followed by "Charles Russell Lowell: 1835–1864," the somewhat ambivalent tribute to Lowell's abolitionist cousin, who "had himself strapped to the saddle . . . bound to death." When the political scene is melded into the world of the poems, both sides of its antithetic, but separately univocal, stances are brought together, and thereby paradoxically resolved. As G. S. Fraser and Kathleen Raine have declared: ". . . The stating of an antithesis with the utmost possible tension . . . does in some sense resolve it."

An analogue of this paradoxical resolution may be found in the mythic circle of the year. The mortal struggle of the year-god and his tanist enacts the dramatic identity of opposites, the mystery of the *coincidentia oppositorum*. When the framing convention of Lowell's *Notebook* enforces the pattern of the circle, and when circles or cycles of various kinds recur throughout the volume, the closure or realization of each circuit corresponds to the ambivalence, the openness of each poem. In the figure of Lowell's circle, art and life combine: they are phases of a single process. In the figure of Lowell's circle, the structure of things is accepted as the structure of ideas. These are the concluding lines of "Reading Myself":

10. Robert Lowell, ["Che Guevara"], in Marianne Alexandre (ed.), ¡Viva Che! *Contributions in Tribute to Ernesto 'Che' Guevara* (London: Lorrimer, 1968), p. 75.

> No honeycomb is built without a bee
> adding circle to circle, cell to cell,
> the wax and honey of a mausoleum—
> this round dome proves its maker is alive,
> the corpse of such insect lives preserved in honey,
> prays that the perishable work live long
> enough for the sweet-tooth bear to desecrate—
> this open book . . . my open coffin. (NBK)

"We are the bees of the invisible," according to Rilke. ("Our task is to stamp this provisional, perishing earth into ourselves so deeply, so painfully and passionately, that its being may rise again, "invisibly,' in us.") But Rilke, as a prophet of this work, was stating it in theory; Lowell is actually doing what Rilke taught. His characteristic tone is anti-romantic. The keynote of the Notebook is the humility of its task. The second poem of the "Harriet" sequence, opening the volume, is typical:

> A repeating fly, blueblack, thumbthick—so gross,
> it seems apocalyptic in our house—
> whams back and forth across the nursery bed
> manned by a madhouse of stuffed animals,
> not one a fighter. It is like a plane
> gunning potato bugs or Arabs on the screen—
> one of the mighty . . . one of the helpless. It
> bumbles and bumps its brow on this and that,
> making a short, unhealthy life the shorter.
> I kill it, and another instant's added
> to the horrifying mortmain of
> ephemera: keys, drift, sea-urchin shells,
> packratted off with joy, the dead fly swept
> under the carpet, wrinkling to fulfillment. (NBK)

To rescue love from the horrifying mortmain of ephemera—this is the task of the Notebook, and its chance:

> After loving you so much, can I forget
> you for eternity, and have no other choice?

The last lines of "Obit," at the very end of the book, come full circle with their composite "you" and connect with the book's ambiguous dedication:

for Harriet

> even before you could speak,
> without knowing, I loved you;

and for Lizzie.

And the opening lines of "Harriet," the opening sequence, move already between the fractional and the Whole in the child's idea of God:

> Half a year, then a year and a half, then
> ten and a half—the pathos of a child's fractions, turn-
> ing up each summer. God a seaslug, God a queen
> with forty servants, God . . . she gave up—things whirl
> in the chainsaw bite of whatever squares
> the universe by name and number.

Coming in Lowell's fiftieth year, celebrating (like Harriet with her fractions) "Half a Century Gone," the *Notebook* is a totally occasional poem. But everything, his whole life work, rides on it.

~ BIBLIOGRAPHY

ALFRED, WILLIAM. *Hogan's Goat*. New York: Farrar, Straus & Giroux, 1966.

ALVAREZ, A. "Robert Lowell in Conversation with A. Alvarez," *The Review*, 8 (August, 1963), 36–40.

————. "A Talk with Robert Lowell," *Encounter*, XXIV (February, 1965), 39–43.

AUDEN, W. H. *The Collected Poetry of W. H. Auden*. New York: Random House, 1945.

————. *Secondary Worlds*. New York: Random House, 1968.

AUERBACH, ERICH. *Scenes from the Drama of European Literature: Six Essays*. New York: Meridian Books, 1959.

BARITZ, LOREN. *City on a Hill: A History of Ideas and Myths in America*. New York: John Wiley & Sons, 1964.

BERMAN, MARSHALL. "The Train of History," *Partisan Review*, XXXIII (Summer, 1966), 457–62.

BERRYMAN, JOHN. "The Dispossessed," in Paul Engle and Joseph Langland (eds.), *Poet's Choice*. New York: Dial Press, 1962.

————. "Lowell, Thomas & Co.," *Partisan Review*, XIV (January–February, 1947), 73–85.

————. *77 Dream Songs*. New York: Farrar, Straus & Giroux, 1964.

BLACKMUR, R. P. *Form and Value in Modern Poetry*. New York: Doubleday & Company (Anchor Books), 1952.

————. *Language as Gesture*. New York: Harcourt, Brace & Co., 1952.

BONAVENTURA, SAINT. *The Mind's Road to God*, trans. George Boas. New York: Liberal Arts Press, 1953.

157

BROOKS, CLEANTH, and ROBERT PENN WARREN. *Understanding Poetry.* New York: Holt, Rinehart & Winston, 1960.

———— (eds.). *Conversations on the Craft of Poetry.* New York: Holt, Rinehart & Winston, 1961.

BURKE, KENNETH. *A Grammar of Motives.* New York: Prentice-Hall, 1945.

CALHOUN, RICHARD JAMES. "Lowell's 'My Last Afternoon with Uncle Devereux Winslow,' IV, 40–43," *Explicator,* XXIII (January, 1965), Item 38.

————. "The Poetic Metamorphosis of Robert Lowell," *Furman Studies,* XIII (1965), 7–17.

CAMBON, GLAUCO. *The Inclusive Flame: Studies in American Poetry.* Bloomington: Indiana University Press, 1963.

CARMICHAEL, STOKELEY. "What We Want," *New York Review of Books,* VII (September 22, 1966), 5–8.

CARNE-ROSS, D. S. "Conversation with Robert Lowell," *Delos,* I (1968), 165–75.

COLLINGWOOD, R. G. *The Idea of History.* London: Oxford University Press, 1946.

DOHERTY, PAUL C. "The Poet as Historian: 'For the Union Dead' by Robert Lowell," *Concerning Poetry,* I (Fall, 1968), 37–41.

EBERHART, RICHARD. *The Quarry: New Poems.* New York: Oxford University Press, 1964.

EHRENPREIS, IRVIN. "The Age of Lowell," in Irvin Ehrenpreis (ed.), *American Poetry.* London: Edward Arnold, 1965. Pp. 68–95.

ELIOT, T. S. "A Talk on Dante," *Kenyon Review,* XIV (Spring, 1952), 178–88.

————. *Selected Essays.* London: Faber and Faber, 1948.

FEIN, RICHARD. "Mary and Bellona: The War Poetry of Robert Lowell," *Southern Review,* I, New Series (October, 1965), 820–34.

FRASER, G. S. "Amid the Horror, a Song of Praise" (review of Robert Lowell's *For the Union Dead*), *The New York Times Book Review* (October 4, 1964), pp. 1ff.

————. *Dylan Thomas.* London: Longmans, Green & Co., 1957.

————. "Unmonotonous Sublime" (review of Robert Lowell's *Near the Ocean*), *The New York Times Book Review* (January 15, 1967), pp. 5ff.

FREUD, SIGMUND. *Civilization and Its Discontents,* trans. James Strachey. New York: W. W. Norton & Company, 1962.

FROST, ROBERT. "The Constant Symbol," *Atlantic Monthly,* CLXXVIII (October, 1946), 50–52.

GRAY-LEWIS, STEPHEN W. "Too Late for Eden—An Examination of Some Dualisms in *The Mills of the Kavanaughs,*" *Cithara,* V (May, 1966), 41–51.

GROSS, HARVEY. *Sound and Form in Modern Poetry: A Study of Prosody from Thomas Hardy to Robert Lowell.* Ann Arbor: University of Michigan Press, 1964.

HARDISON, O. B., JR. "Robert Lowell: The Poet and the World's Body," *Shenandoah,* XIV (Winter, 1963), 24–32.

HARTMAN, GEOFFREY H. "The Eye of the Storm" (review of Robert Lowell's *For the Union Dead*), *Partisan Review,* XXXII (Spring, 1965), 277–80.

———. "Structuralism: The Anglo-American Adventure," *Yale French Studies,* 36 and 37 (October, 1966), 148–68.

HEILBRONER, ROBERT L. "Utopia or Bust" (review of Paul Goodman's *People or Personnel*), *New York Review of Books,* IV (May 6, 1965), 12–13.

HOFFMAN, DANIEL. "Robert Lowell's *Near the Ocean:* The Greatness and Horror of Empire," *Hollins Critic,* IV (February, 1967), 1–16.

JARRELL, RANDALL. *Poetry and the Age.* New York: Vintage Books, 1955.

JOHN OF THE CROSS, SAINT. *Dark Night of the Soul,* trans. E. Allison Peers. Garden City, N.Y.: Doubleday & Company (Image Books), 1959.

JONES, A. R. "Necessity and Freedom: The Poetry of Robert Lowell, Sylvia Plath and Anne Sexton," *Critical Quarterly,* VII (1965), 11–30.

JUNG, C. G. *Aion: Researches into the Phenomenology of the Self,* trans. R. F. C. Hull. New York: Pantheon Books, 1959.

———. *Mysterium Coniunctionis: An Inquiry into the Separation and Synthesis of Psychic Opposites in Alchemy,* trans. R. F. C. Hull. New York: Pantheon Books, 1963.

———. *Psychology and Alchemy,* trans. R. F. C. Hull. New York: Pantheon Books, 1959.

———, and C. Kerenyi. *Essays on a Science of Mythology: The Myths of the Divine Child and the Divine Maiden,* trans. R. F. C. Hull. New York: Harper & Row, Publishers (Torchbooks), 1963.

KUNITZ, STANLEY. *Selected Poems: 1928–1958.* Boston: Little, Brown & Company, 1958.

———. "Talk with Robert Lowell," *The New York Times Book Review* (October 4, 1964), pp. 34–39.

———. "Telling the Time," *Salmagundi,* I, 4 (1966–67), 22–24.

LANGBAUM, ROBERT. "The Function of Criticism Once More," *Yale Review,* LIV (Winter, 1965), 205–18.

LOWELL, ROBERT. "Benito Cereno," *Show* (August, 1964), pp. 82–96.

———. "Buenos Aires," *New York Review of Books,* I (February, 1963), 3.

LOWELL, ROBERT. "Central Park," *New York Review of Books*, V (October 14, 1965), 3.

―――. ["Che Guevara"], in Marianne Alexandre (ed.), ¡Viva Che!: *Contributions in Tribute to Ernesto "Che" Guevara*. London: Lorrimer, 1968. P. 75.

―――. "The Cold War and the West" (a symposium), *Partisan Review*, XXIX (Winter, 1962), 47.

―――. *For the Union Dead*. New York: Farrar, Straus & Giroux, 1964.

―――. "For the Union Dead," *Atlantic*, CCVI (November, 1960), 54–55.

―――. "Four Quartets" (review of T. S. Eliot's *Four Quartets*), *Sewanee Review*, LI (1943), 432–35.

―――. "Fourth of July in Maine," *Atlantic*, CCXVII (March, 1966), 66–67.

―――. "Hopkins' Sanctity," in *Gerard Manley Hopkins*, by the Kenyon Critics. Norfolk, Conn.: New Directions Pub. Corp., 1945. Pp. 89–93.

―――. *Imitations*. New York: Farrar, Straus & Cudahy, 1961.

―――. Interviews. See
Alvarez, A. "Robert Lowell in Conversation with A. Alvarez."
―――. "A Talk with Robert Lowell."
Brooks, Cleanth, and Robert Penn Warren. *Conversations*.
Carne-Ross, D. S. "Conversation with Robert Lowell."
Kunitz, Stanley. "Talk with Robert Lowell."
McCormick, John. "Falling Asleep Over Grillparzer."
Seidel, Frederick. "Robert Lowell."
Time Cover Story on Robert Lowell.

―――. "John Ransom's Conversation," *Sewanee Review*, LVI (1948), 374–77.

―――. *Land of Unlikeness*. Cummington, Mass.: The Cummington Press, 1944.

―――. Letter to the Editor of the *Village Voice*, November 19, 1964, p. 4.

―――. Letter to the Editors of the *New York Review of Books*, X (February 29, 1968), 32.

―――. Letter to President Johnson, *The New York Times*, June 3, 1965, p. 2.

―――. *Life Studies*. New York: Vintage Books, 1959.

―――. *Lord Weary's Castle and The Mills of the Kavanaughs: Two Volumes of Poems*. New York: Meridian Books, 1961.

―――. "The March," *New York Review of Books*, IX (November 23, 1967), 3.

―――. *Near the Ocean*. New York: Farrar, Straus & Giroux, 1967.

―――. "91 Revere Street," *Partisan Review*, XXIII (Fall, 1956), 445–77.

———. *Notebook 1967–68*. New York: Farrar, Straus & Giroux, 1969.

———. *The Old Glory*. New York: Farrar, Straus & Giroux, 1965.

———. "On the Gettysburg Address," in Allan Nevins (ed.), *Lincoln and the Gettysburg Address: Commemorative Papers*. Urbana: University of Illinois Press, 1964. Pp. 88–89.

———. "On Robert Lowell's 'Skunk Hour' " (a symposium), in Anthony Ostroff (ed.), *The Contemporary Poet as Artist and Critic: Eight Symposia*. Boston: Little, Brown & Company, 1964. Pp. 107–10.

———. "On Two Poets" (Ford Madox Ford and Sylvia Plath), *New York Review of Books*, VI (May 12, 1966), 3–4.

———. "The Opposite House," *New York Review of Books*, IV (April 8, 1965), 4.

———. "The Pacification of Columbia," *New York Review of Books*, X (June 20, 1968), 18.

———. "Paterson II" (review of William Carlos Williams' *Paterson* [Book Two]), *The Nation*, CLXVI (January 3–June 26, 1948), 692–94.

———. *Phaedra*, a translation of Racine's play, in *Phaedra and Figaro*. New York: Farrar, Straus & Cudahy, 1961.

———. *Poems: 1938–1949*. London: Faber and Faber, 1950.

———. "The Poetry of John Berryman" (review of *77 Dream Songs*), *New York Review of Books*, II (May 28, 1964), 3–4.

———. "Prometheus Bound" ("derived from Aeschylus"), *New York Review of Books*, IX (July 13, 1967), 17–24.

———. "Prose Genius in Verse" (review of Robert Penn Warren's *Brother to Dragons*), *Kenyon Review*, XV (1953), 619–25.

———. "Randall Jarrell" and "On the Seven-League Crutches," in Robert Lowell, Peter Taylor, and Robert Penn Warren (eds.), *Randall Jarrell: 1914–1965*. New York: Farrar, Straus & Giroux, 1967. Pp. 101–17.

———. *Selected Poems*. London: Faber and Faber, 1965.

———. "Thomas, Bishop and Williams," *Sewanee Review*, LV (1947), 493–503.

———. "Two Walls," *New York Review of Books*, X (May 9, 1968), 16.

———. "Visiting the Tates," *Sewanee Review*, LXVII (1959), 559.

———. *The Voyage, and Other Versions of Poems by Baudelaire*. London: Faber and Faber, 1968.

———. "Waking Early Sunday Morning," *New York Review of Books*, V (August 5, 1965), 3.

———. "William Carlos Williams," *Hudson Review*, XIV (Winter, 1961), 530–36.

LOWELL, ROBERT. Untitled reply to the editors of the *Harvard Advocate*, CIII (Spring, 1969), 17.

MANN, THOMAS. "Tonio Kröger," in *Stories of Three Decades*, trans. H. T. Lowe-Porter. New York: Alfred A. Knopf, 1951.

MARTZ, LOUIS L. "Recent Poetry: The Elegiac Mode," *Yale Review*, LIV (Winter, 1965), 285–98.

MAZZARO, JEROME. *The Achievement of Robert Lowell: 1939–1959*. Detroit: University of Detroit Press, 1960.

————. *The Poetic Themes of Robert Lowell*. Ann Arbor: University of Michigan Press, 1965.

MC CORMICK, JOHN. "Falling Asleep over Grillparzer: An Interview with Robert Lowell," *Poetry*, LXXXI (1953), 269–79.

MILLS, RALPH J., JR. *Contemporary American Poetry*. New York: Random House, 1965.

NEWLOVE, DONALD. "Dinner at the Lowells'," *Esquire*, LXXII (September, 1969), 128–29, 168–84.

OGDEN, C. K., I. A. RICHARDS, and JAMES WOOD. *The Foundations of Aesthetics*. New York: International Publishers, 1929.

OTTO, RUDOLF. *The Idea of the Holy: An Inquiry into the Non-Rational Factor in the Idea of the Divine and Its Relation to the Rational*, trans. John W. Harvey. New York: Oxford University Press, 1958.

PARKINSON, THOMAS (ed.). *Robert Lowell: A Collection of Critical Essays*. Englewood Cliffs, N.J.: Prentice-Hall, 1968.

PEARSON, GABRIEL. "Robert Lowell," *The Review*, 20 (March, 1969), 3–36.

PERLOFF, MARJORIE. "Death by Water: The Winslow Elegies of Robert Lowell," *English Literary History / ELH*, XXXIV (1967), 116–40.

POIRIER, RICHARD. "Our Truest Historian" (review of *For the Union Dead*), *Book Week*, II (October 11, 1964), 1, 16.

POUND, EZRA. *The Cantos, 1–95*. New York: New Directions Pub. Corp., 1965.

RANSOM, JOHN CROWE. "A Look Backwards and a Note of Hope," *Harvard Advocate*, CXLV (November, 1961), 22–23.

————. *Poems and Essays*. New York: Vintage Books, 1955.

————. "Robert Lowell," in Stephen Spender and Donald Hall (eds.), *The Concise Encyclopedia of English and American Poets and Poetry*. New York: Hawthorne Books, 1963. Pp. 191–92.

————. *The World's Body*. New York: Charles Scribner's Sons, 1938.

RILKE, RAINER MARIA. *Duino Elegies*, trans. J. B. Leishman and Stephen Spender. New York: W. W. Norton & Company, 1939.

————. *Selected Letters of Rainer Maria Rilke*, ed. Harry T.

Moore. Garden City, N.Y.: Doubleday & Company (Anchor Books), 1960.

ROETHKE, THEODORE. In Cleanth Brooks and Robert Penn Warren (eds.), *Conversations on the Craft of Poetry*. New York: Holt, Rinehart & Winston, 1961.

————. *The Far Field*. Garden City, N.Y.: Doubleday & Company, 1964.

ROSENTHAL, M. L. *The New Poets: American and British Poetry Since World War II*. New York: Oxford University Press, 1967.

Salmagundi, I, 4 (1966–67). Articles on Robert Lowell by Stanley Kunitz, Herbert Leibowitz, Ben Belitt, Jerome Mazzaro, M. L. Rosenthal, Robert Ilson, and Thomas Parkinson.

SCHOPENHAUER, ARTHUR. *The World as Will and Idea*, trans. R. B. Haldane and J. Kemp. Garden City, N.Y.: Doubleday & Company (Dolphin Books), 1961.

SCHWARTZ, DELMORE. *Shenandoah*. Norfolk, Conn.: New Directions Pub. Corp., 1941.

————. *Summer Knowledge: New and Selected Poems, 1938–1958*. Garden City, N.Y.: Doubleday & Company, 1959.

SEIDEL, FREDERICK. "Robert Lowell," in *Writers at Work: The Paris Review Interviews, Second Series*. New York: The Viking Press, 1963.

SENIOR, JOHN. *The Way Down and Out: The Occult in Symbolist Literature*. Ithaca, N.Y.: Cornell University Press, 1959.

SONTAG, SUSAN. *Against Interpretation and Other Essays*. New York: Farrar, Straus & Giroux, 1966.

————. *Styles of Radical Will*. New York: Farrar, Straus & Giroux, 1969.

STAPLES, HUGH B. *Robert Lowell: The First Twenty Years*. New York: Farrar, Straus & Cudahy, 1962.

STEPHANCHEV, STEPHEN. *American Poetry Since 1945: A Critical Survey*. New York: Harper & Row, Publishers, 1965.

STEVENS, WALLACE. *Collected Poems*. New York: Alfred A. Knopf, 1954.

TATE, ALLEN. *The Man of Letters in the Modern World*. New York: Meridian Books, 1955.

————. "Remarks on the Southern Religion," in *I'll Take My Stand: The South and the Agrarian Tradition*, by Twelve Southerners. New York: Harper & Brothers, 1930. Pp. 155–75.

TAYLOR, PETER. "1939," in *Happy Families Are All Alike*. New York: McDowell, Obolensky, 1959. Pp. 207–46.

THOMAS, HUGH. *The Spanish Civil War*. New York: Harper & Brothers, 1961.

Time Cover Story on Robert Lowell. *Time*, LXXXIX, 22 (June 2, 1967), 67–74.

TOYNBEE, ARNOLD J. *A Study of History,* Abridgment of Volumes I–VI, by D. C. Somervell. New York: Oxford University Press, 1947.

TRILLING, LIONEL. *The Experience of Literature: A Reader with Commentaries.* New York: Holt, Rinehart & Winston, 1967.

WARREN, ROBERT PENN. *Brother to Dragons, A Tale in Verse and Voices.* New York: Random House, 1953.

————. See also Brooks, Cleanth, and Robert Penn Warren.

WEATHERHEAD, A. KINGSLEY. "Imagination and Fancy: Robert Lowell and Marianne Moore," *Texas Studies in Literature and Language,* VI (Summer, 1964), 188–99.

WILLIAMS, WILLIAM CARLOS. *Pictures from Brueghel and Other Poems.* New York: New Directions Pub. Corp., 1962.

————. *The Selected Letters of William Carlos Williams,* ed. John C. Thirlwall. New York: McDowell, Obolensky, 1957.

WIMSATT, WILLIM K., and CLEANTH BROOKS. *Literary Criticism: A Short History.* New York: Alfred A. Knopf, 1957.

⮞ INDEX